THE
AUTOMOTIVE
SECURITY SYSTEM
DESIGN HANDBOOK

No. 1734
$18.95

THE
AUTOMOTIVE
SECURITY SYSTEM
DESIGN HANDBOOK

J. DANIEL GIFFORD

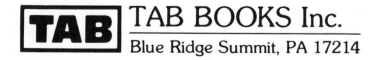

TAB BOOKS Inc.
Blue Ridge Summit, PA 17214

This book is dedicated with love to my mother, of course, but also to her faithful '68 Mustang—stolen twice in one week, but still with her.

FIRST EDITION

FIRST PRINTING

Copyright © 1985 by TAB BOOKS Inc.

Printed in the United States of America

Library of Congress Cataloging in Publication Data

Gifford, J. Daniel.
    The automotive security system design handbook.

    Includes index.
    1. Automobiles—Anti-theft devices. I. Title.
TL275.G49   1985   629.2'75   85-4624
ISBN 0-8306-0734-X
ISBN 0-8306-1734-5 (pbk.)

Chapter art is courtesy of Chapman Industries Corp.

Contents

Acknowledgments

No book is solely the product of a single person, and this one is no exception. I have to say thanks to a number of people who were kind enough to help when help was needed.

My first and biggest thanks to to Teddianne, whose unflagging dedication and willingness to put in a lot of long late hours were the biggest help of all. Randy Allen deserves thanks as well for his production of the photos under some very odd conditions.

Thanks also go to Rodney and Brian of California Radio & TV Supply, for various scrambling around; to Michael P. Steffen of Panavise Products; to Chris Hanlon, for the use of his car; to Tiny's Hamburgers, for sustenance; and last but far from least, to the unnamed company whose word processor was what made this book possible, more or less on time.

Thanks to all.

Introduction

Automotive security has been a problem since probably about 15 minutes after Carl Benz chuffed down a Mannheim street in his three-wheeler in 1887. Automotive crime is a serious problem in this country, and it's growing by leaps and bounds. Thieves are getting more sophisticated, and cars' prices are soaring while we watch—making the incentive for thieves even greater.

There have been many books on security in general, mostly dealing with home and commercial security. Automotive security is by and large an ignored field. If you wanted to protect your car or truck, you either bought a system off the shelf, or you cobbled up something from your electronics bench that you hoped would work. There has been almost nothing published that would help the car/electronics hobbyist build and install a good security system. Many of these books do claim to cover car and truck alarms, but I've found this claim to often be an outright lie. For example, one very popular, respected text on electronic security makes its claim on its back cover, in its jacket blurb, in its preface, and in its publisher's catalog. It *does* cover car and truck alarms—all of one paragraph's worth.

Several books do attempt to present plans for a vehicular security system, as do many magazine articles. These light treatments, however, all make the same mistakes—namely, they tell you how to build the central part of the system (the mainbox), but leave you hanging as to the other parts of the system, sensors, and installation. Nor are these mistakes something of the past; as this book was being wrapped up, an electronics magazine printed a security system article repeating them all.

I really don't mean to deride the existing literature on the subject; it's probably so skimpy because few people have been interested until now. From the stories of rising automotive crime and the booming sales of off-the-shelf systems, I can only conclude that drivers and hobbyists are interested in protecting their cars with their own work. This book is written specifically for automotive and electronics hobbyists who want to design, build, and install their own system in their own vehicle. Hopefully, it provides what's been missing in the automotive security field: concrete design and construction information that lays the groundwork for any average hobbyist to build a security system for a vehicle, be it a simple relay-type system or a fearsome thief-stopper that rivals a computer in complexity.

Believe it or not, this is the first major work ever written on automotive security system design. I could be wrong, but in more than six years of research and design, I never came across one.

The terms "car," "truck," "auto," and "vehicle" are used more or less interchangeably throughout this book. Unless a paragraph very specifically refers to one type of vehicle, the information in it is equally applicable to all types of vehicles—cars, trucks, vans, RVs, buses, semis—and even basically to motorcycles, light airplanes, and boats.

An undertaking of this scope is almost certain to contain errors. Most of the really foolish ones, hopefully, will have been eliminated by the rewriting and editing process, but others are certain to slip through. If you should find any—or if you have any suggestions, comments, or ideas relating to automotive security—I would really enjoy hearing from you. If a revised edition of this book ever becomes a reality, then there would be time to catch the errors, and room for more circuits, tricks, and information—with proper credit to you, of course. Write in care of TAB BOOKS Inc.

With this book and your skills, hopefully you'll be able to create a custom security system for your car (or truck, or van . . .) that will stop thieves and strippers dead in their tracks.

1

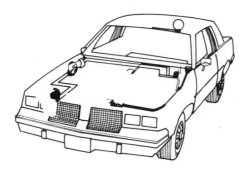

Automotive Security

T HIS IS A HANDBOOK OF INFORMATION THAT YOU CAN USE TO protect your car. The main focus of this book, and indeed the focus of most of the automotive security field, is on electronic security systems. While the electronic systems offer a great deal of protection, it should be remembered that there are some other, simpler approaches to automotive security.

If you aren't sure that you want to get involved with the complexities of electronic systems, you should consider the vast array of nonelectronic options available. Knowing the capabilities of the mechanical and physical protection methods and how they can work alone, with each other, or in conjunction with an electronic system is necessary knowledge for anyone who wants to give his car the best available protection. Also, whether or not you choose an electronic security system for your car's protection, you should learn the basic information of auto security. To be an effective security system designer—using the phrase "security system" in its largest sense, including mechanical and other types of protection—you must understand not only the capabilities of the hardware, but also the different types of criminals and the methods they use to commit their crimes. In other words, you must know the who and why as well the what and how.

Mechanical and electronic devices are not all there is to protecting your car. Some simple common sense can help in the fight to keep your car off of a statistics list; a little foresight in parking, locking, and watching your car can go a long way.

WHO WOULD STEAL MY CAR?

There are many more threats to your car's security than just car thieves. In fact, a complete description of the different types of automotive criminals would fill a book this size!

For our purposes, however, most of the criminals interested in your car will fit into one of the following categories. These categories often overlap or have blurred boundaries, but they are sufficient to give you an idea of what it is you are fighting.

Each type of criminal needs to be countered in a somewhat different way. A well-designed security system, whether mechanical or electronic, can foil them all.

Vandals

The vandal, of course, doesn't need much description. He's only interested in breaking what's breakable, smashing what's smashable, and slashing what's slashable. Vandalism can be casual crime—as when a passerby breaks your antenna or side mirror—or an all-out attack on your car, maybe to get even for some real or imagined slight to the vandal. With car repair and repainting costs soaring, even a casual vandal can cause thousands of dollars worth of damage.

Strippers

If you've ever seen a car in a deserted area with its hood open and wires dangling out, or maybe up on crude blocks and missing its wheels, you're familiar with the stripper's work. A stripper isn't interested in stealing the whole car, but just what parts he can cart away.

He might be stealing the parts for his own use, but it's more likely that he's selling them, either to a fence or to his friends. He might even be renting a flea-market table and selling his thefts to unsuspecting bargain hunters.

If a stripper is clever, fast, and knows what to sell at any given time, he can keep himself supported pretty well. A single set of some types of wheel covers can fetch a thousand dollars!

Smash-and-Grabbers

The smash-and-grab thief is a close relation to the stripper, with one difference. Where the stripper is interested in what's *on* the car, the smash-and-grabber is interested in what's *in* the car.

All smash-and-grab thieves, who are also called auto burglars, use pretty much the same method. The look for valuables inside of the car and then get them by breaking open the door or smashing the window. If they suspect that the trunk or glove box might contain something of interest, it doesn't take them very long to check. A short crowbar can open a trunk even faster than the key.

The smash-and-grab thief can be found almost anywhere there are valuables inside cars: parking lots of expensive stores, high-priced office building parking garages, etc.

Joyriders

A joyrider is the lowest order of car thief. He's looking for a car to steal and cruise around in and maybe to show off to his friends. He'd like to take a nice new sports car, or even a hot Hemi 'Cuda, but if it's handy and has the keys in it, he'll just as soon take a rusty Ford station wagon. The joyrider is only a threat to vehicles that are very easy to steal; if it's locked or doesn't have the keys in it, he probably won't bother.

Amateur Car Thieves

The amateur car thief doesn't steal cars for a living. He may be unemployed, or just underpaid, but he usually just steals cars to supplement his income. He will steal anything that will bring him a few bucks.

The amateur often steals the cars for a more professional organization, like a chop-shop. He could also steal a car and try to sell it, but he has to find a way around the fact that the vehicle doesn't have legal registration papers.

The amateur often has a few simple car-theft skills. He probably can unlock a door and hotwire the ignition, but that's all.

Professional Car Thieves

The professional car thief steals cars for a living, and like other professionals he's very good at his livelihood. Armed with an array of specialized tools and even more specialized knowledge, he can and will steal any car he wants. He can unlock doors, defeat alarms, find and short out killswitches, and do anything else necessary to drive that car away.

The pro usually works in league with a larger organization. The organization can simply be a regular buyer for his cars, or it could even be a regular employer paying him a salary with bonuses!

The pro doesn't steal a car and then try to sell it; he "takes an order" for a specific car and then delivers it. If a buyer or his organization wants, say, a 1979 Porsche 924, red with a black leather interior and Pirelli P7 tires, that's precisely what the pro will deliver. If the auto is going to a private buyer, oftentimes the pro's substantial fee will include legitimate registration papers—in the new owner's name!

An experienced pro with good connections can make more than a thousand dollars a week, and there are those who make even more. All tax-free, of course.

There is one very important point to be remembered about the pro: he cannot be foiled or stopped. If you own the only red '79 Porsche 924 with black leather and P7s in the area, all of the security equipment you can pile into it won't keep the pro from driving it away. The only possibility you have for protecting your car against a professional is to make it so difficult to steal that he'll look elsewhere. Just the same, if for some reason he wants your car, he'll get it. The only positive protection against a pro is paid-up insurance.

WHY ARE CARS STOLEN?

Despite all of the different types of thieves, cars are mostly stolen only for a few reasons. Of course, there is always the unusual case that can't be categorized, but most thefts will come under one of a few headings. As with the thieves themselves, there's a great deal of overlap and blurring of the lines between these categories; also as with the thieves, the distinctions are enough to give you the general idea.

Excitement

The joyrider doesn't steal cars for any financial gain, but just for the thrills. Because auto theft is almost always a felony, it's a pretty big risk. The joyrider likes it that way—to him, the bigger the risk, the bigger the thrill.

Although joyriders usually just abandon the car when it runs out of gas, they'll almost always trash it before they take off. This just adds to their thrills.

Parts

Probably the biggest single reason for the car theft is for the car's parts. Whether it's for the thief's car or for sale, whether the parts are factory or aftermarket, the number of cars stolen for parts exceeds all the other categories put together.

One of the biggest buyers of stolen parts is what is known as a *chop-shop*, an unscrupulous body repair shop that uses stolen parts. A chop-shop may have a full-time pro who supplies the needed parts, or they may use whatever amateurs are around at the time. In either case, the stripped hulk of the stolen car is either abandoned or towed to an obliging wrecking yard where it is crushed into unidentifiable scrap.

From a customer's point of view, a chop-shop works much like any body repair shop. Damaged cars are brought in and duly given written estimates; the insurance company or customer is billed for new parts. For a few hundred to a thousand dollars, a set of stolen parts is ordered instead. Because in expensive cars and/or cases of major damage new parts can cost thousands of dollars, there is an enormous profit potential in chop-shops. Also, since a chop-shop can easily undercut everyone else's prices, they often have all of the business they can handle. Since one painted body part looks identical to another, chop-shops are also very difficult to catch and put out of business.

There is a similar type of operation that deals with mechanical parts instead of body parts. A garage can boost its profits substantially by using stolen parts in place of the new parts that they charge for. While engines have prominent and difficult-to-change identification numbers, transmissions, differentials, steering gear, and suspension assemblies don't. These parts do have several numbers, but very few owners ever record them.

Standard replacement parts aren't the only thing that thieves steal cars for. Custom body, engine, and interior parts are very hot items in most areas. Many cars are stolen in order to be relieved of their aftermarket parts. The thief may want the parts to make his own car look as sharp as the stolen one did, or he can fence them for a handsome profit.

Resale

The other big market for stolen cars is for resale. The amateur will steal any car that's sure to be an easy sale and unload it on someone who's too blinded by the low price to notice the lack of proper registration. Many people aren't familiar with the paperwork involved in a private-party used car sale, and can be duped with any impressive array of legal- or official-looking papers.

Some pros will take advantage of this scam, but more often

they'll change the car's identifying number and register the car legally. With a fair price, a hot car can be sold very quickly—and at almost 100 percent profit! Another trick is to forge a set of papers, sell the car, and then disappear before the purchaser can find out.

One of the most common ways that pros forge a car's identity is by using what is known as a switcheroo, or 'roo. A totaled-out car of a particular make, model and color is bought, perfectly legally, and after a short wait its identifying numbers and paperwork are transferred to an identical but undamaged stolen car. The car is then reregistered as reconstructed vehicle, and the wrecked car is crushed into unidentifiable scrap. 'Roos are very, very difficult to catch.

These methods, even the switcheroo, will only work on cars common enough not to attract attention in their own right. If a thief were to try to forge a set of papers for a Ferrari 512, for example, he'd have a pretty hard time trying to sell it. First of all, there aren't that many 512s in the country and it wouldn't take long for a buyer to check them all out. It would be a bit expensive, but a person putting down around eighty thousand dollars wouldn't mind.

This isn't to say that expensive, rare, and exotic cars aren't stolen for resale; they are. They are stolen for resales out of the country. A ring of pros usually steals a large number of these types of cars in a short time. The cars are then loaded on a freighter and shipped to another country for sale—usually in South America. Legal enforcement usually doesn't exist after the freighter leaves port, because the few law enforcement organizations that have jurisdiction don't have the manpower.

Getaway Cars

Along with the flashier types, a number of dull, inconspicuous cars are stolen for parts, or for resale; they are stolen for use in crimes.

A bank robber or hit man doesn't want a flashy car that witnesses will remember and cops can trail, but rather a nice nondescript family-type car that will blend into the background. One of the most popular groups of cars for this purpose is the mid-sixties Chevrolet. Not only are they common enough to be "invisible," but they often have very powerful engines.

This, as melodramatic as it might seem, is not a TV-only occurrence. It's rare, but it does happen.

STRIPPING, BURGLARY, AND VANDALISM

Strippers and smash-and-grab thieves both regard cars as a sort of mobile self-service store. For the stripper, they are auto-parts stores; for the smash-and-grabber, they are shopping malls. Both types can be found working the same parking lots and garages.

Strippers and Stripping

All cars are potential targets for the stripper. If it's a common model, the parts will be very easy to sell. If it's a more expensive or rare type, the parts will fetch a premium price. Almost all cars have something that will interest a stripper.

The stripper will work any area where he can find cars unwatched or hidden from view. Large, dark parking lots, multilevel garages, or even dark streets are good places for a stripper to ply his trade.

Strippers are very fast; they can have all salable parts off of a car in minutes. A practiced stripper can have a stereo or CB radio out in seconds. The problem with all of this speed is that it multiplies the damage done to the car. If a stereo is stolen from the dash, the console and dash will be ripped apart and the wiring pulled out. If a stripper steals the wheels and tires, the car will often just be allowed to drop, cracking or crushing transmissions, differentials, and brake drums and discs.

A recent phenomenon in automotive crime is the enormous number of stereo thefts from late-model German cars. Audi's, BMW's, and the like seem to be caught in a wave of break-ins. Their large rear vent windows afford easy access for thieves, and they very often have expensive Blaupunkt, Concord, and Alpine stereos. The problem is so bad, both in numbers of thefts and in terms of the damage done to the dashboards, that a number of bizarre things are occurring. According to San Francisco columnist Herb Caen, cars are appearing with license plates and window signs that read NO RADIO, and when drivers call the police to report a theft, the first question they get is "BMW or Porsche?"

Strippers' skills vary, but most aren't stopped by locks or other mechanical methods of protection. If it's in their way, they'll simply break it. However, few strippers have the knowledge to defeat even a simple electronic system.

Smash-and-Grabbers and Auto Burglary

The smash-and-grabber or auto burglar is not particular about what he takes from inside the car, as long as it's valuable. He'll take the purse or briefcase lying on the seat, but he won't ignore the tape recorder or camera next to it. Even a locked door won't stop a smash-and-grabber; his very name comes from his technique of breaking out windows to get the items.

The hot time of the year for smash-and-grab thieves is the Christmas shopping season. Not only are the cars loaded with expensive and untraceable gift items, but often jackets, purses, and other items that got too heavy to carry. Also, people tend to get careless around the joyous holiday season and forget to lock their doors.

Smash-and-grabbers also work in teams, with one partner driving slowly down the rows of cars while the other pops trunks and tosses valuables into their car. A swift team can hit dozens of cars before they are forced to quit. This teamed method also makes for a quick getaway if it's needed.

Vandals and Vandalism

Vandals, when caught, are almost always found to be children or teenagers. They aren't looking for anything except fun or excitement, and if they come upon your car while it is hidden from view, they'll have their fun by destroying whatever they can of it.

Vandalism is a very difficult crime to prevent. Unlike the more serious crimes, vandalism is almost always random and unplanned. Any car, anywhere, can become a victim of vandalism, even sometimes if it is in plain sight. If a vandal is asked why he did it, his answer, likely as not, will be something like, "It seemed like a good idea at the time . . . "

RISK EVALUATION

Once you have decided that your car needs protection, you must determine how much protection it will need. It is important to try to place your car in a risk category, because on the one hand it will save you time and money and on the other hand it may save your car. If you were to overestimate your car's risk, you could spend needless dollars on expensive security equipment. If you were to underestimate, you could lose your car.

Finding a clear-cut status for your car's protection is by no means an easy chore. You must evaluate yourself, your habits, and your car. Once you manage to place your car in a risk category, you can begin the task of selecting your methods of protection.

Common Risk Factors

Many factors of a vehicle's risk aren't readily obvious; some may even surprise you.

If your car is a very common model, it will be popular with all types of thieves looking for parts. Obviously, the more common the car, the bigger a market there is for its parts. There are a number of common car models that have both body and mechanical parts that will interchange over a wide number of years, models, and even makes.

The most common car of this type is the ubiquitous Volkswagen beetle. The Bug can swap engines, transaxles, and other major parts almost universally. In the 30-odd years of its production, the Bug only had three major body changes—i.e., three sets of body parts. Many parts change only cosmetically and will fit in each other's place.

Another car of this type is the mid- through late-sixties Chevrolet. Many of the body parts will interchange not only across broad year lines, but even over to other General Motors makes. The engines and other major mechanical parts are the most standardized: they are almost a universal fit across 10 years and dozens of different cars!

Both the Volkswagen Bug and the Chevys are popular not only with the straight-replacement and chop-shop sets, but also with the hot-rodders. Cheap parts are always welcomed and rarely questioned.

Lately, there has been a resurgence of standardized parts within manufacturers. It is now common for most parts to be shared by half-a-dozen or more models. It vastly reduces design, tooling, production, and inventory costs, but it increases the risk of theft for individual cars.

An example of this late-model interchangeability is the General Motors intermediate line. Although grilles, taillights, and trim are different, many body panels and mechanical parts are identical among all of a car's sister makes. An even more striking example is Ford's *Fox* series: the Fairmont, Zephyr, Cougar, Thunderbird, Granada, Continental, Mustang, and Capri are all derived from the same chassis and mechanicals.

If your car is one of these, or another that has broadly used parts, you should consider a moderate level of security. A high level is not usually needed, since the main attraction to the car is for strippers and amateur thieves. A small amount of protection will be enough to convince such criminals to look elsewhere—and there's probably an identical car quite nearby.

Obviously, if your car is expensive, rare, or high-performance, it is a good target for many types of automotive crime. All types that fall into this group should be given a high level of protection. All types of thieves are attracted to these cars. The joyrider wants something fast and flashy, the better to serve their ego; strippers and amateurs want the parts, because they fetch premium prices; the pros want them because the cars themselves fetch premium prices.

All years of the Corvette fall into this category, both because (again) they have broadly interchangeable parts and because they are highly coveted. All of the true exotics—Ferraris, Lamborghinis, Maseratis, and the like—are in this category as well. It would seem that these types would almost automatically have security systems; however, many of these types' owners trust good will and their insurance to protect them. The joyriders will be stopped by this childishness, but halting the others, particularly the pro, will require topnotch security measures.

Anything that is expensive is also in this group. Jaguar sedans, Mercedes', Rolls', and even Cadillacs and the bigger Volvos and BMWs are prey to criminals because of their cost, and in turn, their parts' cost.

A bit out of place in this pedigreed category, but still a part of it, is the broad group known as muscle cars: the Mach 1s, GTOs, Roadrunners, Superbirds, Shelbys, 'Cudas, Z28s, Trans Ams, etc. These good-looking, popular, high-performance cars are probably one of the most-stolen groups that exist. The ponycars they are based on, too, the Mustangs, Camaros, Firebirds, Challengers, Chargers, Barracudas, and Javelins are all enormously popular with auto criminals. They are popular with the joyriders because there is little that has a hotter image. The strippers love them because they are often loaded with custom and factory parts and speed equipment; both the custom and factory parts bring up top dollar. Both amateur and pro thief alike love them because they are common enough to easily resell, and the class of people that buy them are often starry-eyed enough to overlook the niceties of paperwork.

Everything in this category should be given a maximum amount of protection: up to two or three percent of the vehicle's worth should be spent on security hardware and measures.

There is another factor that applies to all cars, rare or common, old or new, cheap or expensive: how much the car is left unwatched is a primary factor in determining risk.

10

If your car is left on streets, in large parking lots, in multilevel garages, or even out in your own driveway very much, you should increase the amount of protection it is given. Even if the car holds no other attraction for automotive criminals, the vandals will be interested. If the car is of the rare, expensive, or high-performance set, it cannot be given too much protection! An electronic system backed by one or more mechanical devices is definitely the minimum for this type of situation.

Unique Risk Factors

All of the factors mentioned above are general ones, one or more of them is almost certain to apply to your car. The more specific factors cannot be comprehensively listed. There are many that might be almost completely unique to you, your car, or your situation. You will have to extrapolate from the information here to circumstances that may be dangerous only in your area.

Does your car have some special attraction for thieves? Is there a high rate of theft in your area? Is there a high rate of unemployment? Has your model of car been popular with thieves? Do you often have expensive equipment in it, either personal or job-related? Do you have a large number of children in your neighborhood?

If you carefully examine all sides of your situation, using these questions and factors as a guide, you should be able to arrive at a pretty clear idea of how much protection your car will need. Remember that it's better to slightly overestimate the risk than underestimate it at all. Also, a good security setup can add appreciably to a car's resale value.

PROTECTION METHODS

There are probably more ways to protect a car than there are cars. Most of the common methods are listed here, but there's always a new way—and the more unusual or inventive your method, the more likely it is to foil a thief.

Common Sense Protection

A lot of the problems in protecting your car can be handled by using a little common sense. The very simplest and one of the most effective methods of protection is to lock your doors and take your keys. Although this has been heavily promoted by both government and private consumer agencies, many cars are still stolen each year with the keys in the ignition. A car that is locked every single time it is left—even for "just a minute," even in its own driveway—will be safe from many types of crimes.

The other common-sense method of protection is to always park the car where it is brightly lit and visible to numbers of people. In store or mall parking lots, park under a light and as near to a main entrance as possible. In a public lot, park near a busy sidewalk or street. In multistory garages, park where the car is visible from outside by passersby. This technique alone will scare off most thieves, strippers, and vandals. Between these two simple and free methods, a large part of potential automotive crime can be prevented.

Physical Protection

There are some physical modifications that you can make to your car and its accessories that will help protect it. Most of these methods will work best with another type of protection, where they can mutually enhance the car's safety.

If you are forced to leave your car in a deserted area or along a freeway, there is a very simple trick that will help ensure that it's still there when you return. Remove a critical running part of the car, and a thief will be unable to drive it away. The most common variation of this trick is to remove the coil-to-distributor spark wire, as Fig. 1-1 shows. Without this wire, the starter can crank until the battery is dead, but the engine will not start. The wire simply pulls off; hide it in the car or take it with you. Don't forget to replace it when you return.

Unfortunately, this method has been used for so long that some thieves carry a spare spark wire with them as a matter of course. A more effective technique, particularly if the car is going to be left for a few days, is to remove either the positive battery cable or the starter relay. Since both of these parts carry hundreds of amperes, a thief will not be able to jump them with an ordinary piece of wire. Few thieves carry the double- or triple-ought-gauge wire needed. To remove either will require some simple tools, but you should carry a tool kit in you car anyway.

If you like this idea, you can build a removable starter relay. You can either wire all of the connections with quick-disconnects, or mount the whole relay on a removable plug. In either case, make sure that the contacts of the connectors have enough current capacity.

A protection method that will help keep the car from being stolen for either parts or resale is to simply customize its exterior. A set of pinstripes or rally stripes, or a distinctive paint job, will

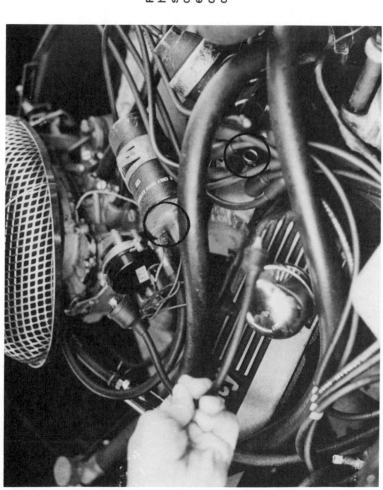

Fig. 1-1. Pulling the coil wire and hiding it or taking it along is fast and simple theft protection for emergency situations. It has lost most of its effectiveness, since some thieves carry a space wire as a matter of course.

make the car highly identifiable, and even individual body parts will be easy to spot. If a car stands out among others, a thief will tend to avoid it. He doesn't want a car that many of the owner's acquaintances and the police will be able to spot.

For more expensive cars and rare models, there is a very effective trick that will stop even a pro. While it is best suited to cars in the more expensive range, it is applicable to all cars. A glass company, using a wax resist and hydrofluoric acid, etches the vehicle's identification number into each and every piece of glass in the car. The numbers are small and inconspicuous and will not affect the car's appearance, but the thief cannot change or remove the numbers in the glass. Because replacing the glass would often cost several thousand dollars, more knowledgeable thieves will simply leave the car alone.

An old grass-roots protection method, and one that is still quite effective, is to wire the vehicle with a *killswitch*. A killswitch is exactly what its name implies: a switch that when turned off, "kills" or disables the car. Properly done, a killswitch can fool even a pro into thinking that the car is defective.

The most common method used for killswitches is to splice a normally-open pushbutton into the starter relay control lead, as Fig. 1-2A shows. Unless such a switch is held closed while the key is turned, the starter will not engage. This is the simplest and safest way to wire a killswitch, but it is also pretty obvious to the more knowledgeable thief what the problem is. If turning the key doesn't provide a response, the experienced thief will look for—and find—the killswitch.

There are two other ways to wire a killswitch, both of which give a more convincing appearance of a faulty engine. They require the relay-type killswitch designs shown in Fig. 1-2B. (In fact, the relay-type is better for all uses.) The first is to wire the relay into the hot lead of either the distributor, or, in electronic systems, the control box. The thief may be able to hotwire the starter, but if the killswitch is off, the engine will not catch. Another way is to wire the relay into the supply wire of an electric fuel pump, if your car has one. When the switch is off, the engine will turn over and even start, but it will only run until the carburetor float bowl runs dry. When an engine starts and then stumbles to a halt, and will not restart, a thief is more than likely to abandon his attempts and not look for any subterfuge.

With either of the last two methods, be extremely careful to mount the switch so that it cannot be accidentally switched off while

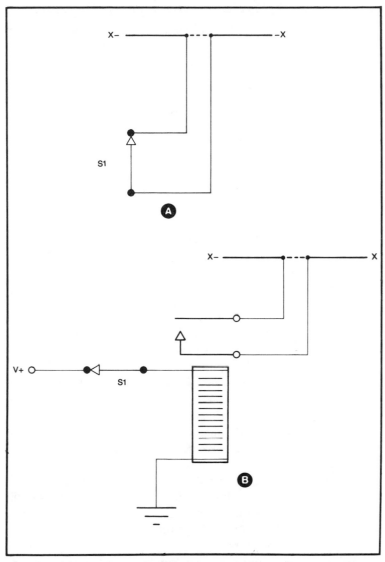

Fig. 1-2. Killswitches are a simple and effective antitheft trick. (A) The simple killswitch is a push-button or toggle switch spliced into a hot lead—which can control power to the ignition, starter relay, or even an electric fuel pump. (B) The relay-type killswitch is a better choice, especially when interrupting a supply line very far from where the switch will be. The added length of wire to the current path will be minimized by putting the actual switching element—the relay—right at the break. The line XX in both schematics represents the broken line; under no circumstances should the wires running from the break to the switch be smaller in gauge than the interrupted wire—and going up a size isn't a bad idea.

the car is in motion. A loss of power on a busy street or freeway could be fatal! With all types of killswitches, the switch should be hidden out of sight. See Chapter 7 for more information on hiding switches.

Mechanical Protection

There are dozens of mechanical security devices on the market. Used alone, in groups, or even with an electronic system, they are highly effective in filling in weak spots in a car's security.

If you have door-lock pulls that are on top edge of the doors, you should definitely install smooth pull-knobs like those in Fig. 1-3. They are very inexpensive and take about one minute to screw on in place of the knobbed factory type. Although they are knurled for easy finger-gripping, they do not have a knob at the top that can be snagged by a wire or coat hanger hook. Since pushing a hook through the window weatherstripping and using it to pull up the knob is the most common method of unlocking doors, this simple and cheap replacement will be very effective. They are absolutely recommended for any and all cars that they will fit, regardless of other security measures.

If you own a car with vent windows, you probably know how easy it is to open them from outside. Often just a wire or piece of plastic will lift the latch; even if the latch locks, a sharp blow from outside will break off the whole mechanism. With the vent open, a thief can reach in and unlock the door. A set of clip-locks on the vent windows will prevent this. Clip-locks are small steel latches that firmly lock the window into its frame. They cannot be undone or broken from outside of the car. Most of the designs do not interfere with normal vent operation.

Even if your car is equipped with an inside hood release, you should consider a hood-locking device. An auxiliary hood lock will keep strippers from stealing batteries and engine parts, and prevent thieves from hotwiring the ignition.

The most common type of hood lock is derived from the special hood-pins used by drag racers, as in Fig. 1-4. These are a set of very strong steel pins that protrude from the radiator support up through a pair of circular steel plates on the hood. Each pin has a small horizontal hole through its tip. In racing applications, as the photo shows, a snap pin goes through the hole to hold the hood down against the stress of a quarter-mile drag run. In a security context, a pair of small padlocks would be used to keep the hood locked.

This type of lock looks good on muscle cars, but on any other

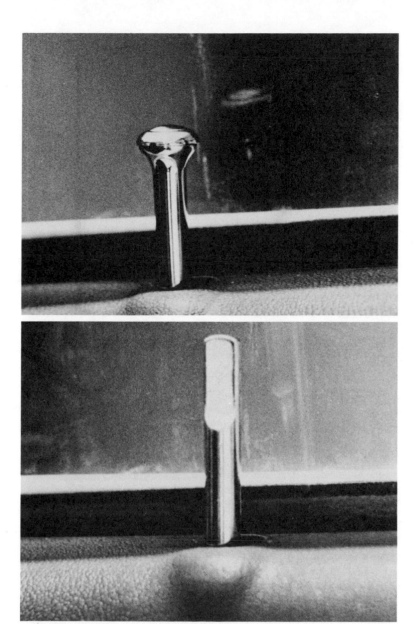

Fig. 1-3. Changing your knobbed door lock pulls for the smooth type is an absolutely required step for all cars that have this type of lock knob. A set only costs about two dollars and takes about one minute to install. By themselves, they will foil so many types of criminals and crimes that they would be worth it even at ten times the price. (Interestingly enough, many auto manufacturers—notably Ford—have now switched over to a smooth "disappearing" type on all of their models.)

Fig. 1-4. Hood locks come in a variety of styles. This type, primarily designed for drag racing, can be converted to security hardware by replacing the lock pins with small padlocks. The locks should have a rubber bumper around their body to keep noise and paint chipping to a minimum.

type of car it looks out of place or even silly. So, there is a less conspicuous type available. In this latter style, a pair of flat circular plates mount in the same location on the hood. In the center of each, and flush with the smooth surface, is a lock cylinder. Underneath, a pin on the lock cylinder twists into a mating recess on the radiator support, securely locking the hood down. This type of lock can be found in a flat black or chrome finish; the flat finish can be painted to match the body color for even less obtrusive installation.

For the fussiest owners and for cars whose looks would be spoiled by any visible type of lock, there is yet another style. The completely hidden hood lock is an assembly that bolts on near the regular hoodlatch assembly. It allows the hood to be opened a few inches, just enough to access the mechanism's keyhole. If the lock isn't opened, the hood can't be opened any further.

If your car is a convertible or other type of open vehicle, there is a mechanism that will be very effective in keeping it where you parked it. This is a long device composed of two steel hooks joined together in the center by a locking ratchet. One of the hooks goes over the rim of the steering wheel and the other is hooked under the brake pedal arm. With it firmly locked together, neither the brakes or the steering will function; the car cannot be driven away. If the wheels are sharply turned to one side and the parking brake is set, the car cannot be towed either. The only way that a thief could move a car so equipped would be with a forklift.

There is another locking mechanism that functions along these lines, consisting of a stepped plate that locks underneath all of the car's pedals. Since neither brake, gas, or clutch can be depressed, the car cannot be driven. It can be towed, though, and if towing is a likelihood, you should use another type of lock.

The great CB radio fad seems to have passed, but these little units are still popular with strippers. Along with the other types of mobile radios, stereos, and tapedecks, CBs can be protected by using a pull-off mount. A pull-off mount, like that shown in Fig. 1-5, is a two-piece mechanism that allows the unit to be quickly

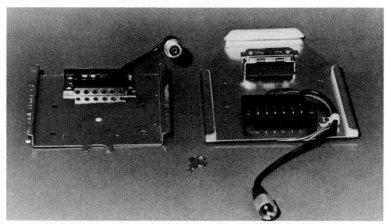

Fig. 1-5. A pull-off mount is an excellent way to mount underdash radios and CBs. The slides and slip connectors can be clearly seen in this photo, along with an unusual feature: a lock to secure the radio into the mount. Nonlocking versions are more common, and cheaper; the lock is too flimsy anyway to stop a thief after he's already in the car.

removed for security. The unit itself is bolted firmly to a plate that has slides along its sides and one half of a set of slip connectors. The necessary wiring from the CB or radio is soldered to the proper terminal of each slip connector, and the vehicle's wiring is soldered to the mating connectors on the base, which is bolted under the dash. When the unit is snapped into place, the slip connectors mate and the unit is wired up. The unit is held snugly in place and only requires a quick yank to pull it free. The unit can be either hidden out of sight in the car or taken along with you.

If you do have a CB radio, you should use a disappearing, demountable, or disguised antenna. CB thieves usually spot their targets by looking for the prominent antennas. If a thief doesn't see one on your car, chances are good that he'll pass it by. Although these antennas do cut the transmitting and receiving ranges somewhat, its better to have a shorter range than no range at all.

The pull-out mount is effective only with underdash stereos and tapedecks. If you have an indash unit, you can still protect it with an Audio Safe™ (Fig. 1-6). Manufactured by Burbank Enterprises, this is a smooth aluminum plate that locks on over the face of the stereo, covering it completely. Because the mounting hardware is also hidden under the unit, the only way that the stereo can be removed is by hacksawing the dash apart. Even then, the thief had better hope that the unit is turned on, and to a station he likes, because the Audio Safe will not come off without destroying the stereo. All in all, an effective method of protecting indash components.

A cheaper and even more clever way to protect an indash stereo is with a little plastic cover called the Incognito. With this five-dollar cap and two pieces of velcro fastener (included), it only takes a second to transform your $500 Alpine into . . . (Fig. 1-7) . . . viola! An instant $49.95 K-Mart special! Cheap and nasty protection, indeed.

If you have invested in a set of expensive wheels and tires, you should also invest in a set of wheel locks. Even some factory aluminum wheels are hot items for thieves: Porsche, Mercedes, and Ford TRX types are all prone to theft along with the aftermarket wheels.

There are two different styles of wheel locks, but they both work in the same basic way. One type replaces a single lug nut on each wheel, and the other, shown in Fig. 1-8, replaces all of the lugs, both with a locking type of lug nut. The locking lug nuts have a very hard, smooth exterior that can't be gripped with a regular lug wrench

Fig. 1-6. The Audio Safe locks on over the face of an in-dash stereo unit, keeping it very secure against theft and vandalism. With the locking cover off, the base plate is almost unnoticeable. A bit expensive, but well worth it if your stereo system is of moderate or high value.

21

Fig. 1-7. The Stereo Disguise is a really tricky way to protect your deck. A $5 plastic cover pops on over your expensive stereo to instantly turn it into a cheapie that even the most hard-up stripper wouldn't bother with. Not as effective as the Audio Safe, since it does not give any physical protection, but very, very effective for the cost.

Fig. 1-8. A good set of locking lug nuts is not expensive and makes it virtually impossible for anyone to remove the wheels without a unique keyed socket. The all-lug type shown here is the better of the two types, and better looking as well. The keying notches can clearly be seen around the bases of the lugs in this photo.

or even a pair of pliers. The lug can only be turned with a special keyed socket. The socket has a pattern that fits into a matching pattern on the base or face of the lug. Only that keyed socket will fit those lugs; don't lose the socket or you won't even be able to change a flat. Interestingly, one of the few recent and effective security moves by an auto manufacturer is Ford's offering of locking lugs on its TRX wheel-equipped models as standard equipment for 1983.

The single-lug type can be chiseled off, or, with the other lugs removed, the stud it's on can be broken off. The all-lug type can also be chiseled off, but it's a very slow process since each tire has four or five lugs; it is almost impossible to break off.

If your car is a low-to-moderate risk, there is a very slick and dirty trick you can use to protect it. The idea is not new, but here it has a new name: "S.H.A.M." This acronym stands for the sham that it represents: Seems to Have an Alarm Mechanism. All of which is a humorous way to say that the car gives the appearance of having an electronic security system. A dummy keyswitch mounted prominently in a fender, with its backside concealed, and a set of warning decals in the side windows is all it takes. A thief will see these and have no way to tell that the car doesn't have a real security system. If the car is of the Volkswagen Bug/sixties Chevy type, the chances are almost perfect that the thief will leave the car alone. This type of sham is not recommended for any type of car that would interest a pro, and it should always be used with another, more positive backup technique.

The most effective vehicle protection, of course, short of a live-in guard, is an electronic security system. The passive locking and other devices can only resist a thief or stripper, but an electronic system can call out for help. The passive methods outlined here are *not* superseded by an electronic system. They are very effective by themselves, and some, like wheel locks, are required for maximum security. All of the passive methods, however, can be used in conjunction with an electronic system, even the best of which can use a little help. Particularly against a professional, an electronic system will be most effective when backed up by a passive device array.

It may well be that one or more of the physical or common-sense methods outlined in this chapter will protect your car or truck adequately, without the addition of an electronic system. If you have decided (or have had it decided for you) that an electronic system is the only way, then the rest of the book is for you.

2

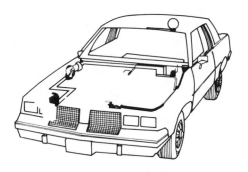

Electronic Security

E LECTRONICS ARE CREEPING INTO OUR CARS SLOWLY BUT surely. For many years, the only electronic device to be found in a car was the radio. Then in 1963 came the first transistorized ignition system; by 1970 a few cars sported electronic ignition systems; by 1980, there was not a car sold in the United States without electronic ignition.

Few other electronic devices have become as universal as the electronic ignition system, but electronic fuel injection, engine-monitoring computers, digital gauges, and cruise controls are becoming commonplace. More exotic and specialized devices crop up daily. Very few of these devices are general-purpose or off-the-shelf items; auto manufacturers and their suppliers are collectively spending billions each year to develop even more sophisticated and specialized versions of these and other devices. Many of these devices use custom-made LSI integrated circuits—in itself no small undertaking, either in terms of time or money.

The use of electronics in automotive security is increasing alongside the more conventional uses, too. With all of the time, money, and development devoted to general automotive electronics, it would seem that electronic auto security would be a high-technology business right along with it. Unfortunately, it's not.

SECURITY SYSTEMS

Electronics have been used to protect cars for a long time. Killswitches, the simplest type of electronic protection, have been used since at least the 1920s, and simple relay/switch/horn-type systems are at least as old. With the advent of the hobbyist-available transistor around 1960, slightly more sophisticated systems began to appear.

With few exceptions that is where the electronic security system has frozen in development—as a fairly low-technology device. The vast majority of commercially-built security systems, even today, do not use more than one or two SSI integrated circuits.

The exceptions are a growing number of automotive security systems available from both auto manufacturers and aftermarket suppliers that incorporate sophisticated digital computer components and specialized sensing devices. While the number of these systems is small, the interest in producing a high-quality system has spread to a number of automotive electronics firms.

Factory-Installed Systems

Over the last two decades or so, a number of diverse auto manufacturers have offered electronic security systems on one or more of their models. Most of those systems have been fairly elementary in design, but increasing automotive crime rates are sparking more interest in better systems among manufacturers.

One of the most widely used applications of a security system as a factory option has been Chevrolet's offering on the Corvette. This relatively simple system, either standard or optional depending upon year, arms automatically and is deactivated via an external keyswitch. In the earlier offerings, the keyswitch was mounted in the left front fender; a later, more sophisticated development integrates the switch into the driver's door lock.

In the exotic-car realm, Ferrari, among others, has offered several different systems at different times, but the variations and small overall numbers preclude any comment.

Recently Cadillac has jumped on the auto-security bandwagon and begun offering an "anti-theft system" on its luxury cars and limousines. This system is approximately equivalent to the system on the Corvette: an elementary auto-protection device.

As an interesting sidelight, motorcycle security systems offered by the manufacturers are fairly sophisticated, using time-delay circuitry and sensitive tilt-motion detectors. In 1982, Honda offered an unusual protection system on its VF750S Sabre. A cable was uncoiled from under the seat, where it was firmly mounted to an armored electronics package, and looped around a convenient tree or pole and locked back into the mounting box. The cable was strong enough to prevent theft by itself, but if an enterprising thief were to cut the cable to steal the bike, he also cut a fiberoptic line running through its center—triggering a hellacious alarm. This innovation is sure to spread, not only to other Hondas but also to other makes of motorcycle.

Probably the most ambitious attempt to provide factory auto protection is not a factory attempt at all. The names Porsche and Ungo Box are practically linked by blood, however. The Ungo Box line of security systems, manufactured by Techne Electronics Limited, were virtually standard equipment on Porsches in the mid through late 1970s. Although their use has spread to many other makes of car, they are still known as "the Porsche alarm." The original TL3000 system (see Fig. 2-1) has been augmented by two other systems and a number of options.

The Ungo is probably the finest automotive security system available over the counter. Not only is it well-designed and easy to use on a day-to-day basis, but it also provides a high level of security and features outstanding precision and quality. Its main drawback is cost: at this writing, a bare-bones Ungo system will run about $300, exclusive of installation. Even at this premium cost, however, the Ungo is a bit incomplete for maximum protection. Although it includes Techne's patented all-electronic motion sensor, a flasher-driven horn, and pinswitches, along with the main control unit and wiring harness, it lacks a backup power supply, a pager, or a high-power siren. (These items are available as options from Techne.)

With the exception of the last, most factory-installed automotive

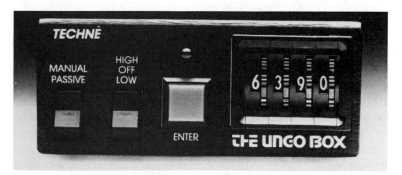

Fig. 2-1. The Ungo Box TL-3000 has for several years been the standard for automotive security systems. Note the switches for selecting manual or passive arming and high/low/off motion sensing; multifunction LED indicator; digital arm/disarm thumb wheels with code entering button. The line has recently been expanded to include the simpler TL-1000 and the very sophisticated TL-4000. Photo courtesy Techne.

security systems are too simple to be effective. This is for several interrelated reasons.

First, any device that must be produced, installed, and serviced by the thousands must necessarily be inexpensive and simple. Car manufacturers just cannot spare the expense and time to build a sophisticated electronic system into each car. The second reason is a corollary of the first: all automotive systems must be simple and very durable to allow for use by unskilled operators. The overall reason that mass-installed factory systems are relatively ineffective is that if a system is simple to install and service, it will be just as simple for a thief to defeat. In fact, with thousands of identical systems about, often on desirable cars, it isn't long before the techniques to defeat them are common knowledge.

The auto manufacturers have the right idea in offering systems as factory options, but they are handicapped by the limitations of their market. Until auto purchasers are willing to pay for quality systems, they won't be offered. Until then, those of use who want top-quality protection will either have to buy an aftermarket system or just build it ourselves.

Aftermarket Systems

There are dozens, if not hundreds, of off-the-shelf automotive security systems available on the market today. It seems that every service station, auto-parts house and discount store has one or more systems on the racks; most auto-stereo dealers offer six or so. While some of these systems are high-quality sophisticated units like the Ungo, the vast majority are elementary systems of doubtful effectiveness. The bulk of these inexpensive systems are one of two types, and although they are produced by dozens of manufacturers, they are all pretty much the same.

The very simplest and least expensive system on the market is the voltage-sensing horn type. This minimal system, often available for less than $20, consists of a siren horn with an electronics module mounted on its back or base. The unit is bolted under the hood and controlled with a hidden switch (or, on more expensive models, a keyswitch) mounted on the outside of the car. A voltage-sensing circuit detects any voltage spikes on the battery's positive lead caused by electrical loads being switched on, such as a door opening and causing an interior light to come on. Either this or a signal from one of the pinswitches guarding the hood and trunk will trigger the alarm; after a set time interval the alarm will reset.

This type of system is a bare-minimum security system and is capable of foiling only the most inexperienced thief. About the only thing in its favor is that it's cheap!

The other common type of security system is a somewhat more sophisticated unit, commonly called a "keyless" alarm system. This type of system is usually available for between $50 and $75, depending upon options and accessories. It has a main control box, or mainbox (usually incorporating a built-in motion detector), a selection of pinswitches, a siren, and a wiring harness.

Once the unit is installed, it is controlled either by a switch under the dash or by a connection to the ignition switch. When the ignition is on, the alarm is off and vice versa. Entry and exit time-delays allow the system to be controlled from inside the car. Like the cheaper system above, this one resets the alarm after a short sound-off period.

While this system is considerably higher in protection, it still does not offer the high quality needed to foil a pro. It is adequate for low- to moderate-risk cars of the VW/sixties Chevy/common-parts type.

What is it that makes the commercially-built aftermarket systems so poor? Several factors contribute to their lackluster performance; most are shortcuts by the manufacturers to lower cost and ease installation by inexperienced buyer-installers.

The first and most common fatal flaw is an overdependence on a single type of sensing. Many systems rely on only a single sensor, usually a voltage-spike detector or a motion sensor, to detect unauthorized entry or tampering. A single sensor can fail or malfunction easily—all systems should use multiple and redundant sensing.

Another common error is single-case construction, where all of the system's functioning parts—mainbox, motion sensor, powerswitching outputs, etc.—are contained in a single box. This cuts costs and eases installation, to be sure, but it also cuts the effectiveness of each part. There is a best location for each different component of a system, and it isn't all under the dash or rear seat. The modular design system, as presented throughout this book, is a far superior method of packaging a system. With the modular system, each component can be duplicated, relocated, or omitted as needed.

The third failing in aftermarket systems is cost: many systems sport high price tags and there is rarely any correlation between price and effectiveness. Some excellent systems are reasonably priced; some very high-priced systems are junk.

Many otherwise good or adequate systems are ruined by gimmickry. The hot selling point of these systems isn't how sensitive or well-designed it is, but rather how clever their gimmick is. Remote controls, combination keypads, keyless arming, and "new and improved" motion sensors are among the more common gimmicks used to prop up sales. It isn't that any of these items are bad in themselves, but they aren't good as a substitute for a proper system, either. A gimmick, no matter how clever or interesting, is not a substitute for a properly engineered system!

Incidentally, the last gimmick mentioned—the "new and improved" motion sensor—is one of my favorites. It seems that every security system offers a "better" mechanical (tilt) (electronic) (super-sensitive) (adjustable) (whatever) motion sensor. This is a prime example of the gimmick as selling point: the aluminum-can type motion sensor, 20 years old at least, is still one of the best means of detecting vehicle motion. With the proper circuitry backing it up, as detailed in Chapter 6, it is considerably superior to many "new and improved" designs.

I certainly don't mean to imply that all commercially-built security systems are poor in quality or effectiveness. Many systems, such as those made by Sleeping Tiger, Clifford, Chapman, or Ungo are top-notch automotive protection. These and other such systems are very high-quality, well-engineered devices, and are particularly effective when installed by a factory-trained installer. Their main drawback is cost: a basic installed Ungo Box will rarely run less than $500, and a full-bore version of some of the others can easily run as high as a thousand! While these systems can be installed by the purchaser, they are far more effective and reliable when installed by a qualified technician. Qualified in this case does not mean mechanics, service-station attendants, or even auto-stereo installers. Qualified means a factory or factory-trained installer. Don't waste your money otherwise. If you want top-quality protection for your car, don't want to do it yourself, and consider price no object, then one of these systems, installed by a pro, is your best bet.

Incidentally, one of these companies, Chapman, has a line of security systems that are among the best I've seen yet. All of their current line of systems (four in all) are built around one of the most brilliant pieces of automotive security engineering yet to appear. A steel casing is bolted under the dash, with a locking pushbutton that resembles a circular keyswitch set into it. A steel tube runs from this casing through the firewall. When the button is pushed in and locked, it pushes a cable through the tube. Under the hood, two things happen. First, a switch attached to the cable activates the alarm portion of the system, and second, the cable activates a deadbolt that locks the hood shut. A high security circular key is needed to unlock the pushbutton.

All of this sophistication (Fig. 2-2) is slightly blunted, though, by two serious shortcomings. First, the systems use the rectangular can-type motion sensor. There is nothing wrong with this type of sensor, especially when backed up with the proper circuitry (not used in the Chapman); however, systems costing this much (a substantial amount) should really offer something better. The second shortcoming is much more serious, and would be in any system: the Chapman systems are not hardwired. Instead of using a direct sensor at each door and the hood and trunk, the Chapman depends on a voltage spike detector on the positive battery cable—a poor substitute at best and one totally unsuitable for any security system costing more than fifty dollars.

Another good point about Chapman's systems is that they are only available professionally installed—the only way to sell such a sophisticated system.

User-Built Systems

The only option for those who want superior automotive protection at a reasonable cost is for them to build it themselves. In many ways, this is the best method.

Fig. 2-2. Chapman's System 800, shown in this diagram, is a very sophisticated security system, but it has its shortcomings (see text). Note in this diagram the unique hood locking/arming assembly, as well as the voltage-spike sensor (on battery cable), the motion sensor (behind/above grille), and the interior-mounted tamperproof pager antenna (rear window). Diagram courtesy Chapman.

While a proper automotive security system is never cheap, by building it yourself you can keep the cost to an absolute minimum and put your savings into an even better system as you go along. A system designed and built by the owner/driver of the car will be truly custom: it will provide exactly the security needed, protect exactly what needs to be protected, and even take into account the foibles and habits of the owner! Using the modular design system in this book, you can create the perfect system for your car.

Also, user-built systems can not only incorporate features found only on very expensive systems, but also unusual and one-of-a-kind features not available anywhere else. Installing a custom-built system is often considerably easier than installing a high-quality aftermarket system. Since you thoroughly understand the operation and function of your system, you can give it a proper installation. With a commercial system, you can often only guess at the best means of installation. (That's why I recommend leaving them to the pros.)

Besides, doing anything yourself is fun, and provides the doer with a great sense of self-satisfaction—and maybe that's the best reason of all!

Legalities

Automotive security systems are legal everywhere, of course, and most law-enforcement officers welcome them. Certain aspects of them, however, can run afoul of city, county, state, or even federal laws. Most of these laws are pretty obvious and straightforward. Some of the most common are discussed here, but if you have any questions, check with the appropriate law-enforcement group. To save some time, if your state has state troopers or a highway patrol, check with their office first. Often these organizations are familiar with all vehicle laws, even county and local ones.

Probably the most widespread type of law that would concern auto security systems is an anti-noise law. These laws can take several forms and may be state, city, or county government administered. Noise level is often regulated by city laws. Some laws may limit the actual number of decibels, and others may define noise limits as an audibility distance. If your area has restrictive noise-level laws, use a legal device to warn passersby and then back it up with a radio pager.

California, Massachusetts, and other states prohibit the use of sirens except by emergency vehicles (fire engines, police cars, ambulances, etc.). This type of law may be found in some counties and cities, too. Check before buying or installing a potentially illegal device.

Many cities and counties have laws requiring alarms to be self-resetting, automatically shutting themselves off within a short time period—usually around 10 minutes. On a vehicular alarm, a reset is a very good idea even if not required by law, since a bell or siren can quickly drain a battery.

Flashing lights are an excellent way to attract attention from passersby and police, and are often incorporated into security systems. Some areas have strict laws regulating what lights can be flashed and how, if they permit it at all. California, for example, permits only emergency vehicles to have flashing lights, but also specifically permits a security system to flash any and all regular vehicle lights to attract attention.

Booby traps are illegal! The use of any device that is designed to kill, injure, or incapacitate a thief is strictly illegal in every state. In addition to being dangerous to yourself, family, friends, and service personnel, devices such as guns, tear gas dispensers, high-voltage units, and explosives can result in prosecution for aggravated assault or premeditated murder. Don't even think about using them!

Did you know that your security system could pay for itself directly? Of course, any system pays off indirectly by keeping your car unmolested and parked where you left it, but there is a more direct (read: pecuniary) payback. Electronic security systems are proven to deter theft and vandalism, and many insurance companies recognize this. As a result, many of these companies offer discounts to drivers who install such systems. These discounts vary, but are usually in the range of 15 percent. If you have even moderate premiums, your system could pay for itself in one premium period! If your insurance company doesn't offer a discount, shop around.

BASIC TERMINOLOGY

The rest of this book is somewhat more technical than these introductory chapters have been; a short discussion of the terminology used from here on in may prove helpful to you. Many of the terms are common electronics terms used in normal context; others are common electronics terms used in special ways. A third group is a set of words coined especially for the automotive security field.

First off, an *alarm* is not a *security system*: the terms are different and have different applications. A security system is a complete mechanical or electronic assemblage that acts to protect a vehicle. It includes sensors, control units, sirens, and all other parts of a vehicle protection device. An alarm is a warning device, either visual or noise-making in character. It is not a term for a complete system: there is no such thing as an "alarm system."

You will run across the term *level* frequently. It refers to a voltage level, and usually to a threshold voltage level. Most of the references are to *high level* or *low level*. High level refers to a voltage very close to the supply voltage of the system or circuit; low level refers to a voltage very close to the negative or ground supply of the system or circuit. Other levels are usually referred to in terms of either fractions or percentages of the supply voltage. For instance, if a particular circuit with a supply of 12 volts triggers at 6 volts, it is said that its trigger level is one-half or 50 percent of the supply voltage. Incidentally, supply voltage is referred to in both text and schematics as V or V+.

Protocol is the system's internal operating language. It is similar to a computer's language, but much simpler. Instead of binary or plain language code like a computer, a security system uses high, low, and intermediate levels, and even pulse inputs and outputs as its language. All of this is referred to as protocol. For example, all of the systems presented in this book (like most systems) require a low-level input as a trigger and respond with a high-level output to activate alarms and disabling units. Some of the more sophisticated units have a control input/output that turns the device off when it receives a high input, and lets the unit function when the control level is low.

A system's protocol must be standardized for the system to operate. The standardization ideally should be taken care of by the design of the system itself; in some cases, where aftermarket devices are integrated into an existing system, it may be necessary to use additional circuitry to "translate" one item's protocol into the other's.

Security systems do not simply turn on and off: they operate in a series of steps or stages. With a simple system, there may be a few as three stages; with a more complex one, as many as six or more. Each stage has a proper name and in some cases may have more than one.

When a system is locked into an off state, where it cannot respond to input pulses, it is *disarmed* or *deactivated*. When it is in an on state where it is ready and waiting for an input pulse to trigger it, it is *armed*. Systems that use an exit delay to allow the system to be controlled from the interior of the vehicle have a stage in between armed and disarmed: *activated*. The system is activated when it is in an on state but is immune to trigger pulses.

When the system is open to and receives a trigger impulse it becomes *triggered*. Generally, triggered refers to the state of a system with an entry delay during the time period between the actual trigger pulse and the sounding of the alarm. In simpler systems with an outside arming control, triggering will refer to the tripping of the alarm.

The system is in the *alarm* stage, of course, when it is actually sounding off bells or sirens, flashing lights, or sending a radio pulse to your beeper. The system *resets* when the reset timer circuit times out and shuts off the alarm. Usually, after the reset, the system returns to the armed state.

If the system incorporates either disabling modules or latching indicators to warn of an alarm state in the driver's absence, the system will remain in an *alert* state until it is disarmed.

These are the most general terms found in this book, but each chapter will introduce new ones. If you stumble over an unknown word, or do not understand a word in a given context, look through the appropriate chapter for a definition.

SYSTEM CAPABILITIES

The capabilities of an automotive security system that you design yourself are unlimited—virtually anything that you can conceive of can be done. The only limiting factor is money.

Anything on, in, or part of your car can be protected, either directly, with its own sensor, or indirectly, with a general area sensor. Outside the vehicle, items such as jerry cans, antennas, skis and ski racks, luggage and luggage carriers, tool compartments, gas caps and gas doors, and other such items can be given protection. Inside, batteries and engine parts, stereos and speakers, CB radios, seats, items in glove compartments and consoles can be protected. Of course, major parts of the car are usually protected by a general-area sensor; wheels and tires, body parts, glass, and custom parts can all be watched over by a properly-designed system.

The system can be automatically or manually controlled with a variety of special circuits and switches. Sensors can be switched in or out or their sensitivity adjusted. The system can be armed and disarmed with any of a dozen types of controls.

The system can foil thieves by using sirens, bells, airhorns, flashing lights, radio paging devices, or by disabling the car.

In short, a system can do anything that you design it to do, and what you design it to do is limited only by your own imagination.

35

3

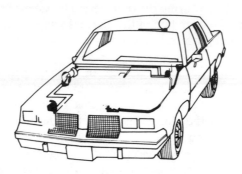

Design Fundamentals

DESIGNING AN AUTOMOTIVE ELECTRONIC SECURITY SYSTEM is very much like designing any other electronic device. You use many of the same parts, tools, and techniques; however, there are differences. An automotive electronic device encounters conditions and situations that no laboratory-bench device would ever come near. In general, an electronic device designed for use in a moving vehicle must be sturdily built, both mechanically and electronically.

Chapters 4 through 8 in this book each detail the design and construction of a specific subsystem of an automotive security system. In each, basic circuits, variations, adjustments, and operation are covered in depth. In addition to this body of specialized design material, there are some general design rules that apply more or less equally to each of the more specialized chapters. So, to avoid repeating these basic rules over and over, they are lumped together here.

To design and construct a top-quality electronic vehicular security system, these fundamental rules must be understood. It must be emphasized that automotive electronics are very different from other types of electronic equipment, and consequently the ordinary rules of electronic design sometimes have little application.

A complex vehicular security system will have many interconnections with the vehicle's electrical system, so an elementary understanding of the functioning of the electrical system becomes necessary.

The basic specifications for electronic components used in an automotive environment are much stricter than for those used in lab-bench construction, and the construction techniques used must be of a very heavy-duty nature: weak components and connections and inferior PC boards and cases will quickly disintegrate in the harshness of the automotive environment.

ELECTRICAL SYSTEMS

The electrical system of an automobile today is essentially the same as one of the 1930s. Some components have disappeared, some have been replaced with more efficient designs, and some have become more sophisticated, but the overall design and function is the same.

Virtually all automotive electrical systems must perform the same three functions. First, there must be a means of generating, regulating, and storing electrical current. Second, there must be a heavy-duty motor and accompanying components to turn the engine over for starting. Finally, there must be a means of creating, controlling, and delivering the ignition spark to the engine's cylinders at the proper time. (In diesel engines, this last system is replaced by a fuel-injection controller.)

Charging System

The charging system's function is to keep the vehicle's electrical system supplied with current. Its main feature is the battery. Automotive batteries are very compact, powerful lead-acid electrical storage units. Most can supply between 50 and 60 ampere-hours of current, and some heavy-duty commercial batteries can supply two or three times that. For the extremely heavy job of turning the starter motor, a car battery can supply 300 to 500 amperes for up to a minute or so. This means that it is supplying as much as 5,000 watts of power, about the same amount as a house draws with all the lights and electrical appliances running!

Although automobile batteries, like most electrical and electronic components, have a dozen or more special ratings, there are only a few that really matter. The first is the already-mentioned amp-hour capacity, which is the overall storage capacity. The second, also already covered, is the battery's cranking capacity, or the peak number of amps that the battery can supply for short periods. Finally, batteries have a reserve capacity rating, which is the number of minutes that the battery can supply 25 amperes before dropping to a specified voltage (usually around 85 percent of peak). Most auto batteries have a reserve rating of 30 to 400 minutes; heavier truck and commercial batteries may have the capability to supply reserve current for 15 hours or more.

To keep the battery charged, all vehicles have an engine-driven generating device. Most cars prior to the mid-1960s have generators that produce dc directly. Generators have several shortcomings, though. First, they must be turned at fairly high rpms in order to consistently produce current. Also, they are heavy; as the electrical demands of automobiles grew, high-current generators were needed. Ordinary generators were heavy; larger ones would have been too heavy. The solution came as the alternator, now almost universal as the vehicular power generator. The alternator produces three-phase alternating current that is internally rectified to produce a smooth high-current dc output at much lower rpms.

The third, and in some ways most important, part of the charging system is the voltage regulator, which performs several critical functions. It regulates the overall voltage of the electrical system; by opening circuits, it keeps battery current from backflowing into the alternator/generator; it controls the charging of the battery by switching the alternator/generator on or off, and it prevents overcharging by keeping the alternator/generator switched off when the battery is fully charged.

The older style of regulator—still in use—is the mechanical type, which consists essentially of three calibrated relays that open and close as necessary. Most newer cars replace the mechanical contacts, which can fall out of adjustment, and arc, burn, and fail, with a solid-state regulator that uses semiconductors to perform the switching. While the latter are more reliable and precise, they cannot be adjusted or repaired and must be replaced if not functioning correctly.

Starting System

When you turn on the ignition key (or press the starter button, on some cars), you engage the starting system. The starter switch, whether it be separate or a part of the key assembly, is a light-duty set of contacts that feed current to the starter relay. The starter relay's contacts are extremely heavy-duty, and carry the hundreds of amps of starting current from the battery to the starter motor. When the current reaches the starter motor, a heavy-duty solenoid pushes the pinion gear of the motor forward into engagement with the flywheel of the engine, and begins to turn the engine. When the engine catches, the pinion gear is retracted, and when you release the starter switch, the motor stops.

Most cars' starter switches have a second set of contacts that act to modify the engine's ignition system during starting. Whether the switch makes a change in an electronic ignition's control module or switches out a standard ignition's coil ballast resistor, the end result is usually to temporarily provide a hotter spark.

Ignition System

The ignition system is responsible for the creation, control, and delivery of the spark to the cylinders. There are two basic types of ignition: the standard type, using a set of contacts or "points" to generate the spark impulse, and the electronic type that electronically generates the spark impulse. The distributor is the heart of all ignition systems; it performs the dual functions of controlling the timing of the spark and the switching necessary to deliver it to the correct cylinder at the correct time.

In a standard ignition, there is a small cam attached to the distributor shaft with either four, six, or eight lobes—one for each cylinder. The lobes open and close the points at precise intervals matched to the rotation of the engine. During the time that the points are closed, a charge builds up in the primary turns of the ignition coil. When the points open, the collapse of the primary-coil field induces a pulse in the secondary turns of the ignition coil. Since the ratio of turns in an ignition coil is 100:1 to 300:1, the pulse is greatly amplified, transforming the low-voltage primary pulse into a very high-voltage secondary pulse of several thousand volts. This pulse is passed back to the distributor cap's central terminal, and in turn to the rotor on the end of the distributor shaft. The rotor is a moving contact; its tip passes from one contact to another along the rim of the cap and passes the spark impulse to the proper cylinder.

In an electronic ignition, the procedure is much the same. Instead of a cam and points, an electronic ignition distributor has a reluctor wheel and a pickup coil. The reluctor wheel replaces the cam; it looks like a spindly gear and has one tooth for each cylinder. As each tooth passes the pickup coil, a very small but precise pulse is generated and passed to the control module. The control module takes this pulse, delays and/or modifies it, and then uses it to trigger a power semiconductor into breaking the primary coil current. The rest of the process is identical to a standard ignition's.

ELECTRICAL SYSTEM CHARACTERISTICS

Despite the mechanical and design differences between individual automotive electrical systems, they all have similar electrical characteristics. These characteristics or parameters must be taken into account when designing your security system. In fact, they will dictate much of the basic design of your system.

Voltage

The voltage of a vehicle's electrical system varies according to the load upon it and as to whether or not the engine (and in turn the charging device) is running. Electrical systems are grouped according to their standing or nominal voltage.

Most cars and trucks built before the mid-1950s, and a few up until the 1960s, have 6-volt electrical systems. This means that the nominal voltage of the system, with no electrical load on the battery, and with the engine off, will measure between 5.9 and 6.1 volts.

By far the most common system voltage is 12 volts. Virtually all cars from the 1960s and all later cars have nominally 12-volt systems—meaning that the battery voltage at rest will be between 11.8 and 12.2 volts. A very few vehicles, mostly heavy trucks and recreational vehicles, have 24-volt systems. If a vehicle of this type doesn't have a 12-volt tap or secondary voltage, designing a security system for it will take special work.

The nominal system voltage is virtually the only voltage level that will affect a properly-designed security system. If the system is guaranteed to be off—with no parts drawing power—whenever the engine is starting or running, the nominal voltage will be the only voltage the system will ever see. If, however, any part of the system will draw power during engine starting and running, certain voltage changes must be allowed for in the design of the system. When the starter motor is drawing power, the tremendous current draw pulls the battery's voltage down three or four volts. Any part of the security system connected to power during starting must be able to operate with this reduced voltage.

At the other end of the spectrum, the electrical system's voltage while the engine is running is 1.5 to 2 volts higher than its nominal level. Again, any part of the security system that's drawing power during the running of the engine must be capable of handling this extra voltage.

The polarity of the system's voltage, in addition to its overall level, is a critical design factor. An electrical system is grounded either positive or negative; the difference depends upon which battery cable is connected to the vehicle's frame as the return lead. If the battery's positive lead is connected to the frame, the system is positively grounded. If the negative lead is connected to the frame, then, the system is negatively grounded. Negative ground systems make up the bulk by far; positive ground systems are fairly rare and virtually nonexistent on new cars. If your car has a positive ground system, be prepared for some extra work.

Current

An automobile battery is capable of supplying an enormous amount of current for a short time, a moderate amount of current for many hours, and a small amount of current for days or weeks. However, the exact definition of moderate and small depends upon the battery, the vehicle, the electrical system, and the condition of each. The better the condition, the more power the battery will be able to supply without running down.

Probably no facet of automotive security system design is more critical than the system's overall current draw. A security system operates 99-100 percent of its time when the engine is off and the battery is not recharging. A stereo or a blower motor that draws several amperes is not much of a strain to a healthy electrical system, since the current it is drawing is constantly being replaced. A security system that operates over a period of days, weeks, or even months is quite a different story. Even though it draws a minimal amount of current, that current is not being replaced and is gone forever when it comes down to starting the car again. If the security system draws too much current, it will run the battery flat prematurely.

When designing your system, keep this point foremost in your mind at all times: **The security system's current draw must be kept to an absolute minimum!**

Noise, Hash, and Voltage Spikes

A dc supply voltage should ideally be absolutely flat and smooth, with no traces of ripple or fluctuation. In reality, even the best lab-bench power supply has some *garbage* in its output. The problem becomes especially severe in an automotive electrical system; it isn't intended to power delicate electronic equipment. Voltage spikes are the worst form of garbage. Like noise and hash, they can cause electronic devices to malfunction; unlike the other two, they are capable of causing severe damage to delicate components.

A *voltage spike* is a short duration—on the order of milliseconds—high-voltage pulse, and can be positive (higher than the system voltage) or negative (lower than the system voltage or even lower than ground) and can reach absolute levels three or four times the system voltage level! Motors, lamps, and the like are unaffected by such spikes: the excess voltage is simply passed on through or short-circuited. Delicate electronic components are more likely to burn out or be otherwise damaged by a voltage spike.

Voltage spikes are caused by a load on the supply line being switched on or off, or by a loose connection. The heavier the draw of the device being switched, the sharper the spike will be.

Noise and hash are similar, related phenomena consisting of regular or irregular pulses on the supply line. *Noise* tends to be single pulses or single frequency pulses; *hash* tends to be white noise—broadband hiss and crackling. It is rare for either type's amplitude to reach the damage-causing level. Instead, noise and hash cause false signals to appear in the electronic device; the most common result in a security system will be a false alarm.

Noise and hash, and for that matter, voltage spikes, are pretty much only generated while the engine is running, with alternators crackling away, switches being flipped, and ignition systems running. However, many cars have electromechanical clocks, electric cooling fans, and engine-monitoring modules that run while the engine is off. All of these can cause garbage, as can loose connections and short circuits in the wiring.

Giving your security system adequate protection against noise, hash, and spikes is absolutely necessary to prevent damage and false alarms. An inadequately protected system, with its endless part failures and falses, will quickly prove to be such a frustration that soon you'll just stop using it.

ELECTRONIC COMPONENTS

Cars are terrible places for delicate electronic components. In addition to the shortcomings of the electrical systems already discussed, extremes of heat and cold, dampness, and vibration will quickly take their toll, destroying inferior components.

The interior of a car parked in hot sun can heat up to 130-140 degrees; the same interior in winter may drop to 20 or 30 degrees below zero. In fact, in some areas of the country, it's not unusual for the temperature to cycle sixty or seventy degrees between night and day!

Dampness and humidity can affect components, too, even those snugly buried in the car's interior. In areas such as the South and Midwest where relative humidities can reach seventy or eighty percent, and in the rainy season anywhere, several problems may crop up. The main problem with humidity is that it can change the apparent values of resistors and capacitors—particularly large values of the former and small values of the latter—by adding a phantom resistance across the device's leads. Timing circuits seem to be particularly vulnerable. The easiest means of humidity-proofing a circuit is to thoroughly spray the finished board with a clear acrylic sealer.

No matter how luxuriously-sprung a car's suspension is, its parts—and its security system—are subjected to almost constant vibration and shocks. Poorly-made connections, weakly supported modules and wiring, and inferior PC boards and fittings will quickly crumble and fail under this torture.

A mobile electronics package of any kind is not a lab-bench piece of equipment that will be coddled and gently treated; it must be strongly constructed of premium parts. There are rigid minimum standards for each type of component, whether it be electronic or mechanical. The use of parts that fail to meet these standards is an invitation to premature failure and erratic operation of your system.

Integrated Circuits

ICs are the heart of nearly every system and subsystem in this book. They are also potentially the most fragile components of a system.

There are virtually only two families of ICs that are usable in automotive security systems: CMOS and linear. The popular TTL series is not really suitable for automotive use; its restrictive voltage requirements and high current draw preclude its use. If you are unfamiliar with the use of either CMOS or linear ICs, you would do well to refer to any good reference book or cookbook on them.

CMOS ICs are excellent devices for automotive security system use. They have wide supply-voltage limits (3 to 15 volts) and extremely low current requirements. In fact, a CMOS IC in a nonswitching mode draws less than one microampere!

In exchange for these two strong advantages, CMOS has a few drawbacks, mainly, low output current. CMOS ICs cannot source or sink more than one or two milliamperes; for higher current output, drivers must be used. CMOS is also susceptible to static-discharge damage; even the small charge in your hand can burn out a chip.

Some simple handling precautions will prevent damage to your

CMOS ICs. First, always keep the ICs pin-down on a metal or conductive-foam surface (conductive foam is rough and black; don't confuse it with styrofoam. Styrofoam can hold a charge more than powerful enough to zap a CMOS chip). Second, never touch the pins of a CMOS IC. Hold it by the ends, and use a DIP inserting tool to plug it into sockets and boards. Third, always use sockets for CMOS ICs in construction, since the tip of a soldering iron can hold a static charge. (In fact, sockets are a good idea for all ICs.)

CMOS ICs come in two different series: the older "A" series and the newer, buffered "B" series. The B series is vastly preferable, since it incorporates static-protection and buffered inputs and outputs, which make its operation more reliable and predictable. The two series are distinguishable by the suffix on their part numbers. No suffix, or rarely, an A suffix, indicate an A-series device. B series units all have a B following their part number.

Linear ICs are available by the hundreds. Timers, op amps, and voltage regulators are the most common types, but special types abound. Most linears have wide supply-voltage ranges, about the same as CMOS, but they draw substantially more current. Fortunately, most of the popular devices have low-power equivalents, most of which are pin-for-pin compatible. For example, the popular 555 timer draws about 5 milliamperes from a 12-volt supply. The Exar XR-L555 is functionally identical (i.e., you can directly plug it in as a replacement for the 555) and draws only about one-third of a milliamp. For even lower-power operation, the Intel 7555 is a CMOS replacement for the 555; it has slightly different operating parameters, but only draws 80 microamperes! It is supposed to be completely static-damage-proof, despite its CMOS makeup. These two lower-power examples are representative of the many types that are available.

All ICs are available in two forms, a plastic-cased mass production unit, and a ceramic-cased industrial/military unit. The plastic units are cheaper and much more common, but the ceramic types are more reliable and have better over-voltage resistance, as well as a wider operating-temperature range. They are difficult to find, but well worth the search. Most good mail-order electronics sources stock an array of the more popular devices in ceramic cases.

All ICs used in automotive systems must have overvoltage and spike protection. The chips are fragile and can be destroyed by even a few milliseconds of overvoltage. Also, most ICs have some provision for noise bypassing; use it!

Semiconductors

Transistors, silicon controlled rectifiers, triacs, and diodes are all used extensively in the circuitry in this book. They are all used as switching devices (as opposed to amplifying devices); the diodes are additionally used as bypassing, regulating and blocking devices. The basic rule to follow when selecting a semiconductor for automotive use is to choose a premium unit.

Transistors have dozens of ratings and specifications, but we only need to be concerned with two. The first is the maximum amount of voltage that the transistors can handle. On the spec sheets, this figure is listed as V_{ce} and V_{ceo}. Most transistors have V_{ce}'s of at least 30 or 40 volts, so this specification is not critical. Anything over 25 volts is adequate. The second rating is the maximum amount of current that the transistor can handle. This figure is usually identified on spec sheets as I_c, or occasionally as I_e. Transistors can have I_c's of 100 milliamperes to 15 amperes or more. Use a device with a current rating above the maximum current that the circuit will demand.

Any transistor that is driving an inductive load such as a relay, a bell, a motor, a solenoid, or a mechanical siren must have a bypassing diode across its emitter and collector. When an inductive load is switched off, a reverse current spike is generated by the collapsing field in the inductor. This voltage, unless bypassed, will destroy a transistor. Remember, a collapsing field in an inductor is the principle that produces an ignition spark!

SCRs and triacs are special-purpose semiconductors collectively known as thyristors. They act as an open switch in a circuit until a small voltage pulse is applied to their gate terminal; they then switch rapidly into conduction and remain in a conducting state until the circuit they are in is broken.

Triacs are primarily designed for use in ac circuits, but they are more flexible than SCRs in dc circuits. An SCR can only be triggered by a positive pulse to its gate; a triac can be triggered by either a positive or a negative pulse. Additionally, an SCR requires spike bypassing much like a transistor, while a triac is inherently immune to transient damage.

Thyristors are available in a wide range of voltage ratings (abbreviated V_{max}) and current capabilities (abbreviated I_{max}). Tiny units for 25 volts and 200 milliamps can be found; heavy-duty stud types are available that have ratings of 1,000 volts at 200-300 amps. Reasonably priced units are available that can handle 200 volts at

6 to 10 amps: these should be adequate for most security system uses.

The smaller-rating devices often have a very low-current-input gate and require only an infinitesimal pulse current for triggering. They are known as *sensitive-gate* thyristors.

The drawback to thyristors, unlike transistors, is that they latch into conduction and the circuit must be broken for at least a few milliseconds in order to shut off. Therefore, they are useless to power such continuous-draw devices as lamps, electronic sirens, and relays, since they would require extra circuitry to break the conducting state.

The great advantage to using a thyristor as a switching element is to use it to power a self-breaking circuit: motorized sirens, bells, even four-way flashers; any circuit that even momentarily breaks its own connections. Why use a thyristor at all? High-power thyristors are available with more current capacity and at less cost than high-powered transistors.

Diodes

Two types of diodes are used in the circuitry in this book: ordinary rectifiers and *zener* or breakdown diodes. Each has several uses. Ordinary diodes have two ratings: the voltage it can carry (V_f) and the current it can handle (I_f). Reverse voltage and current, both infinitesimal, do not figure for the uses they are put to here. For transistor switching and blocking, the popular 1N914/1N4148 diode will be suitable. It has a V_f of 60 volts and an I_f of 10 milliamps. Any similar diode is also suitable.

For bypassing needs and other medium-duty uses, the 1N4001 is a good choice, with a V_f of 50 volts and an I_f of 1 amp. For very heavy-duty use, particularly in power supply blocking, there are a number of "epoxy bullet" diodes with a variety of voltages and I_f's from 2 to 15 amps. For this type of use, any V_f of 25 volts or more is suitable; select the current rating to exceed the maximum expected level of current through the diode.

Zener diodes have two ratings, as well: their breakdown voltage and their wattage. Zeners exhibit a very unusual response when reverse-biased (i.e., when their cathode voltage is higher than their anode voltage). The voltage across the diode cannot rise past the zener's breakdown voltage; if it does, the excess is dumped across the diode, limiting the voltage. The best use of this effect is to use the zener as the heart of a voltage-regulation circuit; bypassing is also an excellent use. Zeners are available with breakdown voltages from 2 to 30 volts in fractional-volt steps and from 30 to hundreds of volts in 1 or 2-volt steps.

The wattage of a zener refers to the amount of power it can dump without damage. They are available from tiny 1/4-watt units to stud-type 100-watt devices. For regulation, 1/2- or 1-watt units are acceptable. For bypassing, 5 to 10-watt units are the minimum and larger devices would not be excessive.

Capacitors

Capacitors have two important uses in automotive security systems: as timing elements and as bypass devices. As a bypassing element, the ratings of the capacitor are generally noncritical; as a timing element, they are highly critical.

The common electrolytic capacitor should only be used for bypassing. It has the advantage of packing a lot of microfarads into a small package at a reasonable price, but its tolerances are loose, its stability is poor, and its leakage is high.

For critical applications (i.e., timing) use only mylar, polystyrene, or solid tantalum capacitors. The first two are available in sizes from a few picofarads up to about one microfarad. Tantalum units are available from 0.1 microfarad to 100 or more microfarads. All three types are characterized by highly desirable parameters: very low leakage, high stability, and close tolerances. (Incidentally, don't confuse "tantalytics" with solid dipped tantalum capacitors; they are improved electrolytics and not up to spec for critical applications.)

In addition to the capacitance of the unit, expressed in picofarads (pF) or microfarads (μF), a capacitor has a voltage rating. This rating is given as the capacitor's Working Voltage, Direct Current, or WVdc. The WVdc is the maximum voltage level that the capacitor can withstand. A capacitor will fail shortly even if its WVdc is exceeded by only a few volts. A capacitor, particularly an electrolytic, working very far beyond its WVdc can explode.

Most polystyrene and mylar capacitors have substantial voltage ratings, often 100 volts or more. Any WVdc of 50 volts or more is adequate for these types of capacitors.

For electrolytics and tantalum capacitors, the question of WVdc is more critical. Not only does this rating determine the voltage at which the unit can work, but to a large extent also determines its leakage rate. Because tantalum capacitors will almost exclusively be used as timing elements, their leakage rate must be extremely low. A tantalum capacitor with a WVdc of 16 volts and a charge of 16 volts will exhibit a much higher leakage rate than one with a WVdc of 35 volts charged to the same 16 volts. For timing applications, use the highest WVdc unit for the given capacitance that you can find.

Electrolytic capacitors have much higher leakage rates, but steps can be taken to minimize this rate. Most electrolytics used in this book are large bypassing units. A 1,000 μF electrolytic being operated close to its WVdc can exhibit a leakage of several milliamperes! Always use a high-WVdc unit electrolytic, particularly with the larger units. Thirty-five to 50 WVdc ratings are the lowest that should be used; if you can find 100 to 200-volt devices, use them.

Resistors

Probably no electronic component is more extensively used than the resistor. High-quality units are very reasonably priced, unlike many quality electronic components. There are four basic different types of resistors.

Carbon resistors are cheap: if you are a high-volume manufacturer, that may be important. However, for the needs of automotive security, they are too loose in tolerance and too low in stability. Avoid them in your construction.

Carbon-film resistors are good-quality units with moderate stability and close tolerances. They are excellent for general-purpose, noncritical use.

Metal-film resistors are very high stability, very close tolerance devices. They are the best resistor that can be bought, excluding very expensive precision devices. They should be used for all critical applications, particularly timing.

For high-power current-limiting applications, wirewound resistors must be used. These somewhat bulky units are cast in either a sand or ceramic case and are generally of low resistance—from a fraction of an ohm to about 100 ohms. Their advantage is their high wattage rating.

The wattage of a resistor is the measurement of the amount of power it can pass without burning up. Most standard carbon- and metal-film resistors are available in 1/4, 1/2, 1, and 2-watt ratings. These units will fill nearly all needs in a circuit, but there are occasions where a resistor may have to pass several hundred milliamperes, which will burn up a small resistor. For this high-power use, the wirewound resistor is used; they are available from 5 watts to more than 100. Of course, any resistor should have a higher wattage rating than it will need; this margin will prevent accidental burnout.

The wattage of a resistor is also related to its temperature stability; the higher the wattage, the more thermally stable it will be. For critical applications such as timing, use an oversized (higher-wattage) unit to keep temperature-related drift to a minimum.

Relays

Relays are perhaps the single most difficult electronic component to find for use in automotive security. To be usable, they must meet a precise set of parameters—and ones that do are few and far between.

Relays, electrically, have two separate parts, so they also have two sets of ratings: one set for the contacts, and one set for the coil.

There is not much use for small, light-duty relays in automotive security; it just makes more sense to switch small loads with solid-state elements. The main need for relays in this field is for heavy current switching that cannot be easily or inexpensively accomplished with semiconductors.

The contacts of the relay are generally rated for a certain current at a certain voltage. Unfortunately, the voltage is usually 120 volts ac, and it is difficult to determine what the current capacity will be at 6 or 12 volts dc. In general, a relay with contacts rated at 10 amps ac will carry 10 amps dc, but there are exceptions. If possible, buy a unit that has a dc current rating for the contacts.

The coil has two parameters: the voltage at which it operates and its resistance, which determines the amount of current that it draws to operate. The voltage of the coil is not difficult to select: simply choose one with a rating that matches your car's system voltage—6, 12, or 24 volts. The coil resistance is far more critical.

Ideally, the coil should have a resistance that will cause it to draw 10 milliamperes or less; this would be 600 ohms for a 6-volt unit and 1200 ohms for a 12-volt. It is difficult, however, to locate relays that have high-current contacts *and* low-current coils. For most uses such as general-purpose power-switching, relays with lower coil resistance can be used. Do not use units, however, that will draw more than 30 milliamps. For any relay that will latch on and remain powered for long periods of time, such as a disabler (Chapter 8), the 10-milliamp figure must be adhered to.

One way to lower the current drawn by a relay is to insert a resistor in series with its coil. Many relays can have their coil current dropped substantially below their usual value and still operate cleanly. This trick can also be used to reduce the system voltage to a value within the relay's coil rating by limiting the coil current to the amount that it would require at its rated voltage.

This resistor is shown in almost every schematic that uses a relay in this book, and it is labeled $R1_{coil}$ in each. Its value, or even its inclusion, should be experimentally determined using the exact components you will ultimately use in the circuit. Some leeway should be left, to allow for slight voltage drops: keep its value at about 75 percent of the maximum it can be.

Derating Components

For maximum reliability and long life, all components in a security system should be derated. Derating means that the part is chosen with load ratings much higher than the actual load it will "see". Some derating figures have already been given, such as the higher-than-needed WVdc figures for capacitors. The greater the difference between the device's rating and actual load, the more reliable it will be and the lower the chances of accidental overload failure. A two-watt resistor that never sees higher than a one watt load is said to be derated by 50 percent; the 50 percent figure is adequate for most components. For very critical and high-power devices, derating of 100 or 200 percent is not an excessive step.

ALARM COMPONENTS

In addition to the ordinary electronic components already discussed, there are a number of specialized components only found in security systems. These parts, too, have strict minimum ratings that must be followed for maximum reliability.

Noisemakers

A noisemaking device is a fundamental part of nearly every vehicular security system. There are dozens of different types available. Sirens, bells, horns, and air horns are all usable. The actual type you select is, of course, up to you, but should meet the standards no matter its type.

For ease of mounting and concealment, the noisemaker should be as small as possible. The more compact the device, the more choices you'll have in selecting a spot for it.

Since the unit will be mounted exposed to the weather and most likely will be underhood, it must be resistant to heat, cold, dampness, oil and gas, and vibration. Ideally, it should be designed specifically for automotive use.

The loudness of a noisemaker is measured in decibels. Most commercially-built devices have their loudness specified either on the package or literature. Read these ratings carefully: their veracity is often highly suspect.

Sound pressure or loudness drops as the distance from the sound source increases. Therefore, the distance at which the device's rating is measured is critical. The honest way to measure the decibel level at a specified distance from the front of the device—usually 10 feet. Figure 3-1 shows an example of an honest rating. Many manufacturers cheat by measuring the sound pressure level directly at the device; even relatively weak devices can produce impressive figures when tested this way. The difference between a measurement at the source and one from ten feet can be ten or more decibels!

Read the manufacturer's rating carefully. If the conditions of test are not specified, and particularly if the unit is inexpensive or the rating seems excessive, the test is most likely at the source. Subtract ten decibels from the given figure to get a reasonably honest figure. Once you have this honest figure, either by calculation or from the package, you can evaluate your selection. A unit with a sound pressure level of 95 decibels or less is simply not a powerful enough device. The sound will be lost within a few feet of the car.

DECIBEL RATING AT
10 FEET IS 90 Db.

Fig. 3-1. An example of an honest sound measurement: the distance from the source is specified right on the front of this bell. Note also the Underwriter's Laboratories certification, always a sign of a well-built unit.

A unit with a rating of 95 to 105 decibels is marginal; it will do for most applications. For maximum distance and protection, do not use a unit with a rating of less than 110 decibels; for a premium cost, earsplitting units with sound pressure levels of 120 decibels can be found.

Another point to consider when selecting your noisemaker is the pitch or tone of the device. Very high or low pitched sounds do not carry well, regardless of the decibel rating sound. A moderately-pitched sound will reach the farthest and consequently will draw the most attention. A bell is a good example of a moderately-pitched sound: think of a firebell, and how its sound cuts through even high levels of background noise. Not that a bell is the only device to use; the principle carries over to moderately-toned sirens and horns, too.

Keyswitches

Keyswitches are, obviously, switches that can only be turned off by the use of a key. They are used as the arming/disarming control in most systems..

There are two basic types of keyswitches: the flat-key type and the round-key type. The flat-key style is usually less expensive, but can be picked or forced fairly easily. The round-key units are virtually tamperproof, and are generally much higher-quality devices. Although either type may be used for interior-mounted keyswitch applications, the round unit must be used in exterior-mount systems and is greatly preferred for all applications. Any keyswitch used as an exterior control must be either weatherproof or be equipped with a spring-loaded, gasketed cover. Figure 3-2 shows both types of keyswitch and the cover.

Sensor Switches

Sensor switches are the small contact switches that are used to monitor the opening of doors, hoods, trunks or the removal of something (toolbox, spare tire) from the vehicle. Virtually any type of push-button switch can be used.

Since sensor switches are usually exposed to some degree to the elements, they must be weatherproof or at least weather resistant. Units designed for outdoor use are ideal, along with any type of "explosion-proof" switch. Explosion-proof switches have all of their working parts sealed in a rubberlike compound, to prevent a

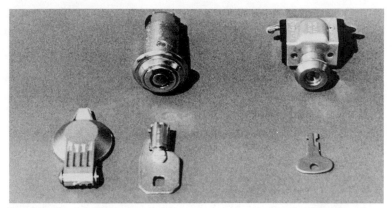

Fig. 3-2. Keyswitches come in flat- and round-key types; the round-key type is superior in all ways but cost. (A type of flat-key keyswitch not shown is barrel-shaped like the round type here.) A spring-loaded, gasketed cover for the barrel types is shown at left; its use is required for all keyswitches mounted outside.

spark from igniting fume-laded air. The seals work equally well to keep out dampness.

Sensor switches must operate reliably many times over the life of the security system, and are usually in a high-stress area. Therefore, any switch used as a sensor must be mechanically very sound. An all-metal unit is the vastly preferred design; a metal bezel is at least required. Plastic-bodied switches are simply not acceptable.

CONSTRUCTION

The construction of an automotive security system is, for the most part, exactly the same as the construction of any other electronic circuit. There are, however, some important differences. As already pointed out, cars are awful places to put any electronic circuitry. Not only are the electronic components themselves subject to the harsh environmental stresses, but the circuit boards and wiring are, too.

Only premium electronic components should be used, and premium construction parts and techniques should be used to join them.

Tools

There are no special tools needed to construct an auto security system; ordinary electronics-bench items will do.

A pair of light wirecutters and a good-quality wirestripper are necessary. These should be separate items, as the combined units rarely work well. There are many inexpensive cutters and strippers on the market, but a few extra dollars spent for a quality piece are not wasted: the cheaper tools lose their alignment and edges quickly.

A light soldering iron with a stand and a selection of solders are of course necessary. A pencil-type iron of 25 to 35 watts is the best size for this light work. Make sure that the iron you select has a fine-point tip: chisel-points and broad-point tips are too thick to do the close-quarters work of soldering ICs into place. A solid, tip-proof stand with a built-in solder sponge is a good idea.

Two gauges of solder will greatly simplify construction, although one will do. A rosin-core 22-gauge is best for very fine, close work, and 20-gauge is better for interconnecting the heavier wires and components. The 22-gauge alone will do, but more inches of it will be needed for the heavier joints.

A small pair of needle-nose pliers can be helpful to pick up tiny components and bend leads and wires with. As with the cutters and strippers, get a quality tool.

A circuit board holder is helpful to keep the board firmly fixed in place while you work on it. There are many types of small vises, third-hands, and clamping devices on the market, such as the Panavise model in Fig. 3-3.

The above items make up a complete basic tool set, but beyond

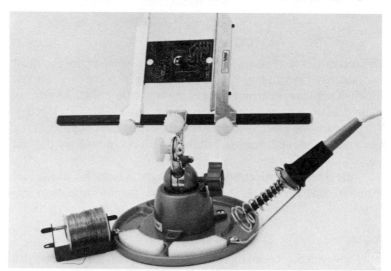

Fig. 3-3. A circuit-board holder is a great help when constructing a complicated board or a large number of boards. A complete work station like this one is about as helpful as you can get. Photo courtesy Panavise.

them are dozens of more-specialized tools that may appeal to you. A look through a good electronics catalog or along the tool aisle of an electronics store will give you an idea of the endless items available.

A bending jig is a grooved strip of plastic or metal that enables you to quickly and accurately bend the leads of components into precise right-angles for insertion into the PC board. When you are constructing a circuit with 50 or 60 resistors, it's a help not to have to stop and bend each set of leads with a pair of needlenose.

A solder-sucker or desoldering tool will come in handy when you need to remove a soldered-in part. For very infrequent desoldering jobs, a roll of desoldering braid is an adequate solution; for heavier or more frequent use, a mechanical hand-held vacuum type is better.

A tool that's helpful for construction work and absolutely necessary for testing, repair, and design work is a good volt-ohmmeter or a multimeter. This is another tool that a few extra dollars will help.

If you prefer an analog (meter-type) VOM, it should have at least 50,000 ohms-per-volt sensitivity and a 4-inch mirrored scale. The overall number of ranges is not important: virtually any meter with the above two standards will have adequate measuring capabilities.

If you prefer a digital multimeter, the only critical factor is its current-measuring ability. Most digitals can only measure up to 200 milliamperes, which is not high enough for many needs. Select a unit with a 2-ampere range, or get a high-current-measuring shunt attachment with the DMM.

These are only a few of the specialized tools available. Once again, a look through a good tool catalog or down your electronics store's tool aisle may turn up something that—for you—will be invaluable.

Techniques

There are a number of basic electronic construction techniques that can be used to build automotive security components. Some are difficult, others are simple; the exact technique that you use will depend upon the circuit, its intended mounting location and use, and, not least, your own skills.

The neatest and most professional construction technique is to use a printed-circuit board. High component density, ease of troubleshooting and repair, and high reliability are only a few of the advantages of using a printed circuit. The drawbacks are that it is a difficult technique at best, particularly with a complicated circuit and more particularly if you are inexperienced in making PC boards. If you want to use PC boards in your system and aren't experienced, there are a number of good manuals and kits on the market; your best move would be to use one or both as a start.

Probably the best technique short of a PC board is to use perfboard and wire-wrap wiring. Even a comparative novice can use this technique to turn out high-quality circuits. The individual components are inserted into the perfboard (use 0.1 × 0.1 drilled board, cut to size) and the leads interconnected with wire-wrap wire. There are several types of wire-wrapping tools available; select one that fits your needs. The joints should be soldered after wrapping is completed. Note that integrated circuits installed in this type of circuit construction must have wire-wrap sockets for proper installation. Be sure to follow the wiring guide or schematic very closely and frequently doublecheck your work. A trick that might help to speed the work and prevent errors is to make a photocopy of the schematic you're working from and trace each connection with a felt pen as you make it. You'll know at a glance what's been done and what still needs to be done.

For very simple circuits, such as the powerswitches of Chapter 8, lug-strip construction can be used. A multipoint lug-strip is used as the foundation of the circuit, with the components and tie-wires soldered between the lugs. Interconnection wires are simply soldered to the appropriate point as well. For a very simple circuit, a circuit board is a waste: lug-strip construction will be easier and cheaper.

A *potted* circuit can either be a separate form of construction or an advanced form of one of the others. A potted circuit has all of its working components cast into a solid block of plastic material or potting compound. The only protruding parts are the interconnection wires or a terminal strip.

Using potted-circuit construction as a stand-alone means of building a circuit works best with low- to medium-complexity circuits. The circuit is constructed as an open framework, with the components themselves and the leads and interconnection wires forming a web. Flimsy by itself, this web gains all of its strength from the block of potting compound it is cast into.

For more complex circuits, the open framework style will be clumsy and fragile; these circuits must be constructed on a regular PC board before potting. When potting a circuit board, make sure that the underside of the board is cast into a block along with the component side. Actually, if a circuit board is being constructed specifically for potting, a number of common construction rules can be thrown out. For higher density and simpler wiring, components can be mounted on both sides of the board; long connection wires do not need to be snugged down or tied to the board for support; small components can simply be soldered from point to point instead of being poked through the board in the usual manner. Remember that there are good reasons for avoiding these shortcuts in normal construction. These shortcuts should only be used when the circuit is to be potted.

Potting a circuit has many advantages, particularly in an automotive system. First, the circuit will be completely impervious to moisture, humidity, and even splashes of water. Also, in a properly potted circuit, vibration will virtually cease to be a problem: with each component tightly locked into place, along with its connections, even a weak joint will be immune to vibration failure.

Probably the main reason for potting a circuit is to prevent unauthorized duplication or decoding of the circuit. If the circuitry is sealed into an opaque plastic block, no one will be able to figure out how it functions—or, in some cases, even what it does! This may become important if the circuit or subcircuit is mounted in an exposed or prominent position, and particularly if the potting is used to hide some proprietary circuit or wrinkle that you'd like to stay proprietary. In electronics circles, this trick is jocularly referred to as "patent by 3M."

There are many compounds that can be used to pot a circuit, some designed specifically for that and some not. If the compound you are using is one not specifically designed or formulated for circuit-potting, make sure that it has a high dielectric constant. Commercial potting compound has a dielectric constant of many megohms per millimeter, and thus won't short out portions of the circuit or change apparent resistances. If you are using another substance, be sure to check its dielectric constant by casting a small block of it and then measuring its resistance with a digital multimeter across a very small gap. If the meter doesn't indicate a resistance of 20 megohms or more, the compound isn't suitable for use as a potting compound.

A potted circuit should always be sprayed heavily with a silicone or acrylic spray sealer to aid in combatting humidity problems.

One final note on potting circuits; make absolutely sure that the circuit is functioning correctly and is properly adjusted before it's encased in the potting compound! Adjustments and repairs are impossible once the block is cast.

No matter what technique is used for construction, there are several points that apply to all of them. Circuit boards used in automotive electronic construction must be of the glass-epoxy (G-E) type; they are usually blue or green and bear a type number G10 or G11. A similar type, possibly better for automotive use, are the otherwise-identical fire-resistant FR4 and FR5 types. The glass-epoxy boards are also highly resistant to damage from vibration and temperature extremes. The tan and brown phenolic boards are plastic-impregnated paper and are too weak for automotive use.

All connections must be made according to the strictest rules. Each connection should be tight and mechanically sound prior to soldering; never depend on the solder to hold the joint together. Use a clean soldering iron and just enough solder: weak and "cold" joints will fail.

All wires should be supported. Short wires usually are self-supporting, since their ends hold them down against the board. Longer wires should be tied off to a support or woven through the board to give them support. A long wire left unsupported will either break or pull loose from its connections due to vibration.

To sum up: use premium construction techniques, tools, and parts. The extra time, money, and trouble will pay off well both in the short and long run.

The final step in constructing your automotive security system is packaging it. Potted circuits are already packaged, but all others need a case to protect them and facilitate mounting. Metal, plastic, and combination boxes and cases are available in hundreds of styles, sizes and shapes. Some have PC board mounting provisions built it, some have knock-outs for wiring, and some are weathertight. Careful searching through catalogs, stores, and surplus houses will probably turn up exactly the case you need.

The components and circuit boards should be firmly mounted inside the case, either with screws or adhesives. Many styles of cases have one or another built-in means of securing components: slots or stand-offs are two common types. If the case you select doesn't have such built-in mounting provisions, you'll have to do some fabrication. Z-shaped strips that fasten to the corner of the case under the cover mounting screw are one trick. If the case is plastic, you can glue the components into the bottom of the case. Use a thick epoxy or "liquid-rubber" adhesive, in generous amounts.

To facilitate installation, all of the input and output leads from and to the internal circuitry should be routed to a lug-strip mounted inside the case. Either a screw-type or a solder-lug type may be used. If a screw-type is used, it will require the installation of lugs or terminals on the system's interconnection wires and the use of lockwashers. The screw types are easier to install when working in a cramped area, but they can vibrate loose. The solder-type connection strips are superior because they cannot vibrate loose, but they can be tricky to connect when working up inside a dashboard or other tight location.

All wires should be connected internally; no wires or lugstrips should be external. The connected wires should be routed out of the case through a grommet. Ideally, all cases should have their seams and grommet holes caulked with a silicone-based caulk to keep out moisture and dust. All cases that will be mounted outside of the passenger compartment must be caulked.

4

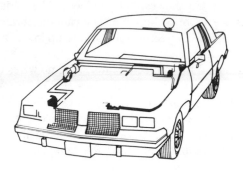

Power Supply

W HEN YOU BUY A COMMERCIALLY-BUILT AUTOMOTIVE ELEC-
tronic device, such as a CB radio or a stereo, all problems
with voltage regulation, spike suppression, and noise filtering are
taken care of internally, by the unit. Your only worry is finding a
convenient power lead to hook the thing to!

When you design and build your own automotive electronics,
however, it's up to you to provide regulation, filtering, and bypassing where needed to maintain proper operation. This is important
in noncritical devices such as a windshield-wiper delay; it is mandatory in such highly sensitive and critical devices as security
systems. In an auto stereo system, a burst of noise or a voltage spike
on the power supply lead will mean at most a crackle or pop from
the speakers. With an automotive security system, that same burst
or spike—or even a much smaller one—can mean a malfunction, a
false alarm, or even a damaged component.

By removing these problems at the source and adding protection to all sensitive modules and circuits, the security system can
be made that much more sensitive without the problem of false
alarms. In turn, it will mean that much more protection for your car.

POWER REQUIREMENTS

Every user-built automotive security system is different. Even those
built unvaryingly from the schematics in this book will have minor
differences from unit to unit. Very small differences in design, con-

struction, component selection, and even installation can mean big differences in operation, sensitivity, and power supply requirements.

A simple relay-type system with a high trigger threshold will be far less sensitive to noise and spikes in its power supply than will be a complex, multi-IC type. In general, then, the more sensitive and complex a system, the more rigid its power supply requirements will be.

Voltage Requirements

Automotive security systems, like most other low-voltage electronic systems, have fairly narrow voltage requirements. They are usually designed to draw a minimum of supply current, and as a consequence even a slight undervoltage may mean that internal components fail to get adequate current. On the other hand, overvoltage of even a few seconds' duration can mean the burnout of an unprotected IC or semiconductor.

For most systems, the supply voltage must remain within 10 percent of the nominal supply voltage. For a 12-volt supply, the level should remain between 11 and 13 volts; for a 6-volt system, between 5 1/2 and 6 1/2 volts. Voltage fluctuation beyond these limits may cause different forms of malfunction in different types of components. Some components may be strongly affected by even slight changes in the supply level, while others may remain unaffected by even wide voltage swings.

Components such as resistors, capacitors, and inductors are virtually voltage-independent. Undervoltage will not affect these parts directly, but may have secondary effects: timing periods may be changed, frequencies may vary, and output circuitry may fail to supply sufficient current. Overvoltage, for the most part, will have just as little effect directly upon these components. Since most resistors carry very little current in normal operation, a slight increase in voltage will not raise the current to a harmful level. Current-limiting resistors are another story, though: if they are operating close to their rating already, an increase in current may burn them out. Capacitors are unaffected by overvoltage as long as it does not exceed their WVdc. If the voltage should exceed the rating, failure of the capacitor will result. Inductors are insensitive to overvoltage, although the accompanying excess current will burn them out.

Relays, paradoxically, can be both insensitive and highly sensitive to voltage fluctuations. Since a relay electrically has two separate parts—the coil and the contacts—each reacts differently to varying voltage. For most automotive security uses, relay coils are chosen for high inherent resistance or have a series resistor to limit their current draw. If the voltage should drop even slightly, the coil may have insufficient power to make the contacts operate, and overvoltage may make the relay operate too soon. Overvoltage can also damage the contacts: the excess current can burn or pit the contact surfaces, or in extreme cases, even weld them together.

Semiconductors such as transistors, diodes, and thyristors need a closely regulated voltage supply for proper operation. Undervoltage can change the bias characteristics of a diode or transistor, and may cause a thyristor to drop out or fail to operate. Thyristors are relatively immune to overvoltage, but can be triggered into premature conduction if the voltage is too high.

Integrated circuits are very sensitive to voltage variations, much more so than discrete semiconductors. The tiny etched chips of silicon can be burned out by a few milliseconds of overvoltage.

The vast majority of ICs used in automotive systems will be either CMOS or linear, and while these families of ICs can operate over a wide range of supply voltages, fluctuations can still cause failures. Once an IC is designed into a circuit using a specific voltage, changes in that voltage can foul up its operation. The IC itself will probably continue to operate, but its input and output characteristics will be changed. Most ICs require certain levels at their inputs to cause the IC to operate, and if either the input voltage or the supply voltage is shifted, the input may be read incorrectly. Undervoltage can cause the chip to have insufficient output drive; overvoltage may increase the device's dissipation to the burnout point. All in all, the power supplied to any circuit or module using ICs should be very carefully regulated and conditioned.

The polarity of the voltage supply is not usually a problem after construction and installation. During these two steps, though, be sure to use great caution to avoid the application of reverse power. Even an instant of reverse current could totally destroy the entire system. During construction, double-check the polarity of ICs, semiconductors, and polarized capacitors. During installation, disconnect the system battery and double-check the connections before applying power.

Current Requirements

Obviously, any electronic system that is operating is drawing current; the question—especially in automotive security systems—is how much current. A well-designed automotive security system may draw as little as 10 microamperes while on standby; the same system in the alarm state, using high-power output devices, may draw as much as 10 amps!

To clearly explain the current requirements and limitations of auto security systems, a typical system's draw at different points in its operation is here broken into four categories. Not all systems will draw current as described in each category, but all possibilities are covered.

> *Note: The current-draw figures given here are only applicable to vehicles with electrical systems in good condition. If your car or truck has a weak system, even a security system within these limits may drain the vehicle's battery.*

Standby current is the power that a system draws while it is on and waiting for a trigger impulse. This category of current draw is perhaps the most important one for the designer to consider. The security system may spend hours, days, or even weeks in the standby mode, and therefore its standby current draw must be minimized as much as possible. Remember that most electrical/electronic automotive devices operate exclusively when the engine is running and the battery is being charged, and that a security system is the exact opposite, drawing current almost exclusively when the engine is off. If the standby current draw is too high, the battery will be drained in short order.

The optimum level for standby current is 60 milliwatts or less: 5 milliamperes with a 12-volt system, and 10 milliamps with a 6-volt system. A security system that draws less than 60 milliwatts will be able to operate virtually indefinitely.

If the system will never under any circumstances be left without running the engine for more than two or three days, then the standby current level can be raised to as much as 200 milliwatts. This amount of current draw can drain the battery, though, and the two or three day limit must be adhered to.

Operating current is the power that the system draws while actually in the alarm state—with sirens, bells, pagers, flashers, etc. operating. While all current draw should be minimized, operating current can be substantial without any penalty. Since most systems will only remain in the alarm state for three or four minutes, a heavy current draw can be tolerated since it averages out to a low figure over time. Lead-acid batteries have considerable capacity to bounce back from a short, heavy draw; in fact, they can withstand a short, heavy drain better than they can a long, moderate one, even if both current drains are equal in the total amount of power drawn.

Parasitic current during the alarm state should be minimized, however. Ten or 100 milliamperes being used to drive a relay or for other nonproductive action are to be more begrudged than a full ampere actually driving an alarm output.

Post-alarm current is the power drawn by the system after the alarm period ends. For simpler systems that do not have any latching indicators or disabling devices, the post-alarm figure will be the same as the standby figure. If the system does incorporate such indicators or disablers, the current that they draw should be added to the standby current figure to obtain the post-alarm current figure.

Determining an acceptable maximum figure for post-alarm current depends heavily upon how quickly you will respond to an alarm state and reset the system, thus disengaging the latched devices. If the car is essentially left untended and an alarm state may not be attended to for any length of time, the post-alarm current should not be appreciably higher than the standby current level. If, on the other hand, you will respond quickly (within an hour or two) to an alarm, the post-alarm current level can be considerably higher—up to 500 milliwatts, if necessary.

Maximum current, like post-alarm current, may not apply to all systems. For simpler systems, the maximum current may be the same as the operating current. For the more complex systems, where modules operate in sequence rather than concurrently, the figure may be imaginary. In either case, the maximum current figure is the amount of current that the system would draw if all components were drawing current simultaneously. This figure, whether real or imaginary, should be used to design and define the limits for the power conditioning circuitry and (if used) the backup power supply.

With most electronic systems, automotive types included, it is standard practice to insert a fuse in the supply line or lines of the system. With automotive security systems, however, this practice should be avoided. While this is a radical step away from conventional safety procedures, it is for a very good reason. If, for example, the fuse to the car's stereo should blow, it means doing without music for a short time. If the fuse supplying power to the security system should blow, however, it means that your car is—unknowingly—left unprotected. You could easily be fooled into thinking that the car was safe, only to return to an empty parking slot.

Instead of a fuse in the supply line, use extremely careful design procedures throughout the system to prevent overloads and short circuits. Follow the common-sense installation guidelines given in Chapter 10.

Noise and Spike Suppression

All sensitive electronic devices are subject to problems from noise, hash, and voltage spikes generated by the power supply. Automotive security systems are no exception.

The more sensitive and complex the system, of course, the better its filtering and bypassing must be. The simple relay-based system could be adequately protected by minimal power supply conditioning; a more complex IC-based system would require a much cleaner power supply for proper operation.

POWER CONDITIONING

It should now be clear that voltage regulation and power conditioning are necessary for a security system to operate properly. The next step is to understand the techniques used to combat power supply problems, and how to implement them.

There are many ways to filter and power supplies, and in fact there are many excellent books on just that subject alone. However, most of these books deal exclusively with plug-in, line-current-powered supplies, and ignore the design of the type of power supply needed for an automotive security system: high current capability with low standby current drain.

The techniques described here draw heavily on ordinary power supply design techniques, but there are some differences—primarily dealing with reducing the amount of current that the regulation circuitry itself draws.

There are at least two different ways to accomplish each desired effect, and each way has its own advantages and disadvantages. By understanding all of the methods and their quirks, the proper method can be chosen for each situation.

Filtering

Regulating the voltage is the final, critical step in providing a clean power supply. Not all components require a regulated voltage supply, but they do require a supply free of noise and spikes. Taking a step backwards along the power supply line, we come to the filtering circuitry that feeds both these components and the regulating circuitry.

Regulating circuitry can only handle only so much noise at its input: if the spike is too large or the noise too strong, it will pass right through the regulator to the circuitry. The filtering circuitry has the job of removing these spikes and noise from the power line. Unlike regulating circuitry, filtering circuitry is fairly inexpensive; there's no reason not to overprotect the system with a well designed filtering array. You can't filter the supply too much.

There are three basic techniques used to filter power lines, and each can be used alone, with another, or even as a group.

The simplest and most effective filter is a simple capacitor across the bus lines, as shown in Fig. 4-1A. A large electrolytic capacitor simply connected in such a manner is a very formidable barrier to spikes and noise. When a spike with an amplitude higher than the nominal voltage comes along, the cap acts as an electrical "pit" and swallows the excess voltage. When a spike with a level less than that of the nominal voltage reaches the terminals of the cap, it acts like a short-term battery and fills in the extra voltage. A capacitor isn't perfect—it can't keep the voltage precisely level—but it can go a long way towards making little dips out of big spikes and bursts of noise.

The WVdc of a bypass or filter capacitor should never be less than three or four times the nominal voltage. If the system is 12-volt, the WVdc of the filter capacitors should be at least 35 to 50 volts—and higher is definitely better.

The capacitance of a filter capacitor can be determined by using a simple rule of thumb: it should have one thousand microfarads for every ampere of current flowing across its terminals. This applies both to large systems filtering capacitors and to small on-card bypass units. If, for example, your system will draw a maximum of 5 amperes, the system filter cap should be at least 5000 μF. If the mainbox draws a maximum of 50 milliamperes, its on-card bypass capacitor should be rated at 50 μF.

Another effective but less common filter element is the inductor. An inductor is a wound coil placed in the power supply line, as shown in Fig. 4-1B. To a dc current, it appears "invisible," presenting just a very small resistance. To a voltage spike or noise, though, it becomes a very solid barrier. When a voltage change passes through an inductor, the coils act like an autotransformer and generates a reverse electromotive force that counters the voltage change. Like the capacitor, the inductor isn't perfect at eliminating spikes and noise, but it's still quite effective.

The primary rating of an inductor is its current capability: since

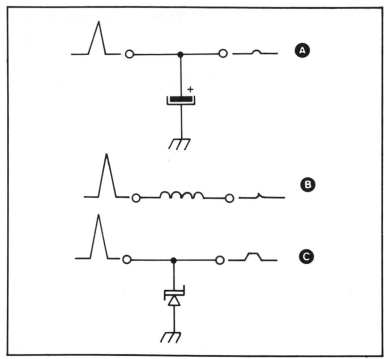

Fig. 4-1. Filtering and bypassing elements. (A) An electrolytic capacitor connected from V+ to ground will flatten out spikes and eliminate most noise. (B) An inductor in series with the V+ supply line will eliminate large spikes. (C) A zener diode connected from V+ to ground will clip spikes at the V_z level, and prevent the voltage from rising past V_z. See text for values to use.

all power that it conditions actually passes through it, it must have enough current-handling ability to keep from limiting the flow or even burning out.

The other measure of an inductor is the amount of reverse current it can generate, measured in millihenries. For most automotive security purposes, use an inductor with a rating of 10 to 20 millihenries. Inductors with high-millihenry ratings and high current capability are hard to find, and you may end up having to wind your own. If you do, refer to any good electronics handbook for details.

Both capacitors and inductors are what is known as *passive* filter elements. They don't take any active role in changing the voltage level, they just react to a change. The third type of filter element is an *active* device that acts on a voltage change instead of just reacting, such as the zener diode.

The zener makes a very effective filtering element when properly used. As Fig. 4-1C shows, it is placed across the bus lines, like a capacitor, and when an excess voltage reaches its terminals, it dumps the excess to ground. Obviously, to filter out some of the heavy spikes that may reach it, the bypass zener must be a pretty hefty device.

The voltage rating of a bypass zener should be about 25 percent higher than the nominal voltage of the system. For a 6-volt system, then, the bypass should be about 7 1/2 to 8 volts; for a 12-volt, about 15 to 16 volts.

The wattage of the bypass zener is determined by the same type of rule as the capacitance of the filter cap: by the number of amperes flowing across its terminals. Five watts per ampere is the minimum. For a system bypass zener with 5 amps flowing past it, then, a 25-watt rating would be the minimum. Although an on-card bypass zener would be a very small device by the rule of thumb, it is best not to use less than a 2-watt device.

High-wattage zeners are hard to find items; you'll have to look around to find the one you need. It is definitely a good idea to use the highest-wattage device that you can find or afford, particularly for system bypassing.

One way to create a high-wattage zener for filtering heavy noise and spikes is to use an ordinary 1- or 2-watt zener to drive the base of a heavy-duty PNP transistor, as shown in Fig. 4-2, thus forming a *shunt regulator*. The shunt regulator will act exactly the same as a simple zener bypass, but with a hundred watts or more of bypassing power. The zener's voltage should still be about 25 percent higher than the nominal voltage, and the transistor should be heatsinked.

A similar bypass element, although very hard to find, is the 1N60XX-series transient voltage suppressors. These act much like zeners, but can handle momentary loads of 1500 watts. If you can find an appropriate-voltage TVS, it's definitely a superior choice over the zener.

Within limits, all three of these bypassing elements can be used together in any combination. The best protection is afforded by a string of all three: an inductor, then a capacitor, and then a zener (Fig. 4-3). For maximum system bypassing and filtering, this triple threat technique is the only way to go. For on-card use, inductors are not particularly effective; a capacitor, a zener, or both is a better choice. The minimum should be a capacitor, and then a zener and capacitor, and only then an inductor.

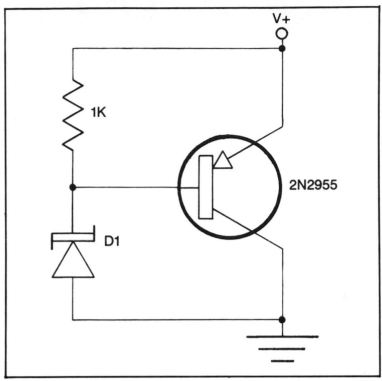

Fig. 4-2. A shunt regulator can solve the problem of locating a suitable high-wattage zener for use as a bypassing element, and give a huge amount of bypassing power. The zener D1 should be a 1-2 watt device, and the transistor must be heatsinked.

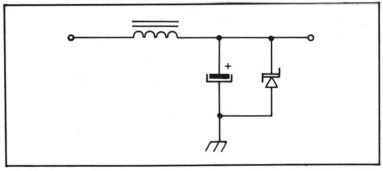

Fig. 4-3. An inductor/capacitor/zener (or shunt regulator) combination will virtually eliminate all spikes and noise from the power line, even very long-duration and large-value ones. This triple-threat protection is best suited to system filtering use.

Whatever you use, it's worth repeating: you can't protect the system too much!

Voltage Regulation

To regulate a system's voltage means to tightly hold it within a predetermined set of levels. The primary function of the regulation circuitry in an automotive system is to limit the upper level of the voltage to a safe point. There is no way for a regulator circuit to boost its output voltage if its input voltage falls below a minimum point, so it is the responsibility of the designer to ensure that the battery and backup power supply have enough capacity to keep the voltage up. This is the primary reason for careful limiting of the security system's current draw: a system with a dead battery is worse than no system at all.

There are two types of voltage regulators that can be used in an automotive electronic system, each with a different regulating element as its heart: the *zener diode* regulator and the *integrated circuit* regulator.

The simple zener diode-resistor network shown in Fig. 4-4 makes an excellent low-current regulator. For one small circuit or part of a circuit that needs an odd voltage level, the simple zener regulator is an excellent choice. The only drawback to it is that it cannot source more than about 20 milliamperes.

For higher current, combine the R-Z network with a *pass transistor*, as shown in Fig. 4-5. The voltage that passes through a pass transistor is regulated by the resistor-zener junction at its base. The current that it passes, though, it is only limited by its own current rating and to some extent the value of the R-Z network resistor. For uses up to one hundred milliamperes, it is okay to select the value of the resistor to limit the output current. For higher current applications, from one hundred milliamps up to two or three amps, use a bias resistor that passes sufficient current to saturate the pass transistor's base and then use a second power resistor to limit the output current. In fact, the two-resistor design is preferable for all uses, low-current ones included.

The main drawback to using a zener as a regulating element is that it is a little bit sloppy, not as precise as it might be, and slow to respond to fast transient voltage changes. For more-precise regulation, the solution is an integrated circuit regulator.

The LM309-XX and 78XX series IC regulators are available in a wide range of fixed voltages, with the most common being 5, 6, 8, 10, 12, 15, 18, and 24 volts. The "XX" in the part number

70

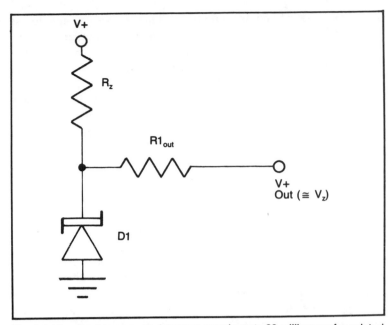

Fig. 4-4. The simple zener regulator can supply up to 20 milliamps of regulated power with only three components. The zener should be a 2-watt unit, R_z should limit the current through the zener to an acceptable level, and the output resistor, in combination with R_z, should limit the output current to the needed level. A small heatsink for the diode (a strip of copper twisted around its body with the ends fanned out is excellent) may be needed in some situations.

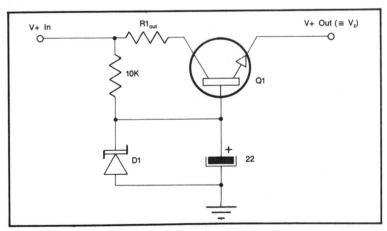

Fig. 4-5. The zener-pass transistor regulator can supply up to 2 or 3 amps of regulated power. The transistor should be heatsinked and the output limiting resistor should keep the output current at a safe level. The zener can be a 1- or 2-watt device. For high current levels (over 1 amp), the capacitor can be increased to 50 μF or more for better stability.

represents the voltage, from 05 to 24. They are very simple to use three-terminal devices, the three terminals being input, ground, and output. All that they require for operation (Fig. 4-6) is one capacitor from their input to ground for filtering, and a 1 μF solid tantalum capacitor from their output to ground for stability.

There are three case styles that the regulators can be commonly found in: the TO-3, TO-220, and TO-92 or −92+. For simple stand alone use, the TO-3 style is recommended. It can directly source up to 1 1/2 amps of regulated voltage, and while the plastic bodied TO-220 is electrically identical to the TO-3, the all-metal TO-3 has better heat dissipation characteristics and is therefore superior for our needs.

If more than one and one-half amps of current is needed, the IC regulator can be used with a pass transistor, too, as in Fig. 4-7. When used with a pass transistor, the IC only needs to handle a few milliamperes, just enough to drive the transistor. Therefore, the expense and current drain of the larger TO-3 and TO-220 regulators are not needed. The TO-92 cased regulators have the same precision regulation as their larger counterparts, but can only directly source one to two hundred milliamps. This is adequate for a small regulation circuit in place of a zener, or as the heart of an IC-pass transistor regulator.

The problem with regulated power supplies is that as their cur-

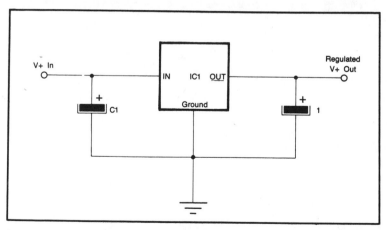

Fig. 4-6. An IC regulator needs only two capacitors to make a complete regulation circuit that can source up to 1 1/2 amps. C1 should be fairly large if the regulator is any distance from the system filtering circuitry. The output capacitor must be a solid-tantalum unit. Most IC regulators have automatic overload protection, but it would be a good idea to add a current-limiting resistor to the output to keep the current below the IC's maximum.

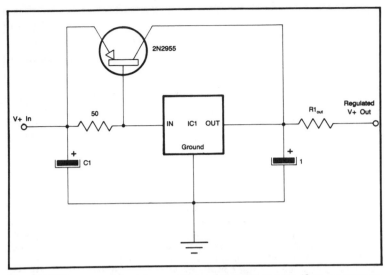

Fig. 4-7. With a pass transistor, an IC regulator can source 10 amps or more of regulated current. The pass transistor must be heatsinked, and the limiting resistor on the output is required to keep the transistor from burning out. The input resistor must have sufficient wattage rating to handle the input current to the IC.

rent capability goes up, their cost skyrockets. There are two techniques to keep the cost of an automotive security system power supply down. If the entire security system has only one module or part that requires a regulated voltage (such as a mainbox), then it is needless to build a powerful system-wide regulated power supply. Bells, pagers, sirens, and relays don't require regulated voltage, and there is no point or gain in supplying them with such.

If the system has only one or two parts requiring regulated power, use a small on-card regulator built into the modules themselves. The zener-pass transistor or TO-92 IC stand-alone type will usually suffice.

Even if the system has a number of components that require regulated voltage, there is no point in building a power supply that will feed all components regulated power regardless of need. The solution is called split-sourcing; literally, the power supply is split into several sources to which the individual components are connected to as their needs dictate. A single-voltage, split-source power supply like that shown in Fig. 4-8 has three different outputs: dirty, filtered, and regulated.

The dirty output simply comes directly from the battery or backup power supply, and is used to power such brute-force devices

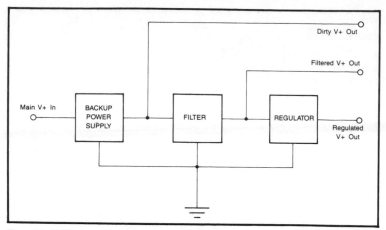

Fig. 4-8. Split-sourcing is the way to keep power-supply costs reasonable. By drawing power for output devices from the dirty output, for powerswitches and the like from the filtered output, and for mainboxes and input circuitry from the regulated output, each stage can be made smaller and thus cheaper. Some very heavy-draw output devices could pull power from the main battery, taking the load off the backup battery should it ever come into play.

as bells, flashers, sirens, and the like. The filtered output comes off after the despiking and filtering section of the power supply, and is used to power such nonsensitive components as power switches and disablers. The final stage, the regulated output, comes after the filtering stage and delivers clean, regulated power to power mainboxes, input circuitry, and other such sensitive parts of the system.

The dirty supply's output current rating is most limited by the capacity of the battery and backup power supply. Ten or even 20 amps can be drawn off without the cost of expensive filtering and regulation circuits.

The filtered output can be made to source up to five or six amps without spending an excessive amount of money on filtering circuitry. The regulated output should not have to supply more than about one ampere of current, well within the limits of a stand-alone TO-3-cased regulator IC. A properly built split-source regulation system will greatly reduce the cost of providing each component with its needed allotment of clean power.

The voltage rating of the regulator circuit will depend upon several factors. For the most part, the regulator's output rating should be equal to the vehicle's nominal electrical system voltage. In other words, a 12-volt system should use a 12-volt regulator, a 6-volt system a 6-volt regulator, and so on. The problem is that all regulators have slight internal losses, and thus their output voltage will be slightly less than their input. For most fixed regulators to deliver their rated output voltage, they require an input at least 1 1/2 volts higher. Therefore, as the chart in Fig. 4-9 shows, when a regulator is used with an input voltage more or less equal to its rated voltage, its output will be about one volt lower than its rating. As was mentioned, the primary function of a regulator in an automotive context is to limit the upper level of the voltage. For most of the circuitry in this book, the slightly lowered voltage will not make any difference in their operation.

The advantages to operating a regulator with its input equal to its rating is current: a regulator so operated draws very little stand-by current.

The exception to this rule is when building a system for a vehicle with a 24-volt electrical system. Parts and components for 24-volt use are difficult to find, and it's best just to circumvent the whole problem by using a regulated 12-volt power supply. Some parts, such

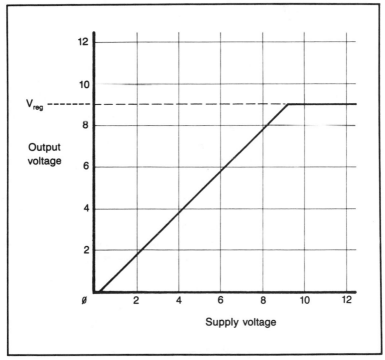

Fig. 4-9. When a regulator circuit has a supply voltage lower than its rated output voltage, the output will lag behind the input by 1/2 to 1 1/2 volts until the supply voltage reaches a sufficient level. This should not affect most systems' operation.

as relays and bells and sirens, can be found in 24-volt configurations. If you can, use these versions of these high-current devices, and use the regulated 12-volt supply for the electronics only. There is an advantage to the 24-volt noisemakers: they're usually a good deal louder than their equivalent 12-volt counter-parts.

Voltage Polarity

In the last chapter it was explained that vehicles have their electrical systems grounded either negative or positive, and that positive-grounded systems are rare.

Nearly all off-the-shelf equipment, and all of the circuitry in this book is designed for negative-ground vehicles. If the vehicle you are designing the system for is a positive-ground, you have several options.

The entire security system can be designed or redesigned from the ground up as a positive-ground system. You will have to know what you are doing, as this step isn't as simple as it sounds. In addition, large components such as pagers and sirens are hard to find in positive-ground form.

Another choice is to use a polarity/voltage inverter. Radio Shack and other companies make them: they turn +6 volts or −12 volts into +12 volts. For the most part they aren't usable for a security system, since they draw a lot of standby current. They are also difficult to use with such a scattered and multipart device, since all connections and cases have to be carefully isolated from the chassis.

There is one true solution to the problem of a positive ground vehicle: make it a negative-ground one. This is not a minor undertaking, but it is well worth it in the long run. If you've owned a positive-ground vehicle for any length of time, you know what a hassle it is trying to find parts and equipment for it, not to mention service. If you're interested in switching your car's polarity, there are a couple of books on the subject, and positive-ground cars are rare enough that one of them probably covers your particular model. Barring that, look for a good British-car garage. Many Jaguars, Triumphs, and MGs are positive-ground, and a good shop has probably done at least a few conversions. If they can't do the work, they can at least give you advice and guidance.

BACKUP POWER SUPPLY

Think about this: what happens if your battery gives out and you're forced to abandon your car in a deserted area? The security system will be useless.

And think about this: a common method of defeating security systems is to snake up under the front of the car and cut the battery cables. Once again, the security system is useless.

In both of these cases, a backup power supply for the security system would be necessity, not a luxury. A backup power supply is a simple, reasonably priced, and valuable addition to any security system.

The heart of a backup power supply is a special type of battery called a *gel-cell* (Fig. 4-10). Like the main battery of the car, a gel-cell is a lead-acid battery. The difference is the electrolyte; instead of a liquid acid, the gel-cell has an acid gelatin as an electrolyte. The advantage of a gelled electrolyte is that it can't leak or spill, and the battery can be mounted in any position. The gel-cell is a compact, powerful source of electricity.

The gel-cell is available in both 6 and 12-volt sizes, with capacities of from 1 to 25 amp-hours. If your security system has a minimum of high-powered alarm equipment, you probably get by with an 8 to 10 amp-hour cell. If your system draws any substantial amount of current, don't use less than a 15 to 24 amp-hour unit.

The cell should be mounted in an inaccessible location inside the vehicle, such as up inside the dashboard or in the trunk. The simple circuitry shown in Fig. 4-11 allows the cell to float-charge continuously from the main battery, prevents it from draining back

Fig. 4-10. Gel-cells are compact yet powerful sources for a backup power supply. Their gelled electrolyte cannot spill, and with simple circuitry, they can be continuously float-charged from the vehicle's main battery and cut in instantly when needed.

into a dead electrical system, and allows it to cut in instantly if the main battery goes dead or is cut out of the circuit. The diodes D1 and D2 must have sufficient voltage and current ratings to handle the full load of the security system—and a sharp derating factor applied. R1 should be chosen to allow the gel-cell to trickle charge at the manufacturer's suggested rate (which usually will be stamped right into the case).

POWER DISTRIBUTION

The final problem with an automotive security system's power supply is mechanical rather than electrical: distributing the power to a number of widespread components can be difficult, particularly when a number of heavy-gauge power leads are needed. The solution: a busbar.

A busbar can be made very simply from a flat copper or steel bar, as Fig. 4-12 shows, by soldering a heavy-gauge lead from it to

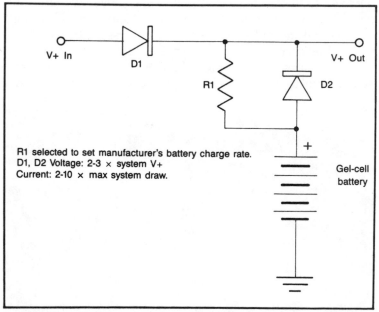

R1 selected to set manufacturer's battery charge rate.
D1, D2 Voltage: 2-3 × system V+
Current: 2-10 × max system draw.

Fig. 4-11. The backup power supply charging and cut-in circuitry is deceptively simple. The security system will normally draw power through D1, and the gel-cell will float-charge through it and R1. When the main power supply is cut out or drops to too low a level, the backup battery will automatically cut in and supply the system through D2, while D1 will prevent the gel-cell's power from draining off to the dead main electrical system. See text for details on the values of D1, D2, and R1.

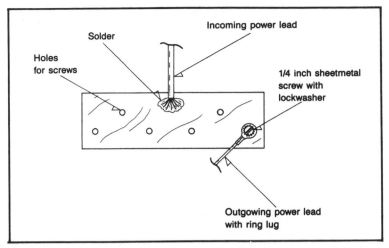

Fig. 4-12. A bus bar can greatly simplify the problems of attaching a number of power leads to a single source. Flat 1/4-inch copper stock can be used; solder the incoming power lead to it and use sheet metal screws to attach the outgoing power leads. The entire unit must be encased in a heavy plastic case to prevent shorts.

the output of the main power source or the output of the backup power supply (if used). An adequate number of spaced holes are drilled in the bar, and sheet-metal screws are used to attach the ring-lugged ends of the individual outgoing power leads. To ensure maximum safety, use lockwashers on each screw and encase the entire busbar assembly in a sturdy plastic case to prevent shorts. Remember, an auto battery stores an enormous amount of current, and a shorted heavy-gauge lead could easily start a fire. Use caution when connecting and routing all of the power leads.

5

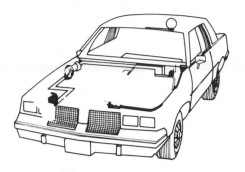

Mainboxes

A T THE HEART OF EVERY AUTOMOTIVE SECURITY SYSTEM, no matter how simple or complex, is a main controller and switcher called a *mainbox*. The mainbox can be nothing more than a relay and a few ancillary components, or anything up to a very complicated device utilizing a dozen or more ICs and a hundred discrete components.

The mainbox is unquestionably the single most important component of a security system. All inputs from controls and sensors are routed to it, and all outputs, whether alarm or indicator, stem from it. The amount of care taken with its design and construction really cannot be overdone. A good mainbox can remain the heart of a system as it grows and expands with your imagination and budget, and it can unfailingly remain in service for years. A poorly built mainbox, on the other hand, will become such a frustration than it will quickly destroy any confidence you may have in your system, and you will discontinue using it.

The mainbox should be designed, redesigned, and overdesigned using premium, heavy-duty design techniques. The importance of such superdesigning cannot be overestimated. Further, the mainbox should be built using only premium components and topnotch construction techniques: military-spec ICs, soldered-wire-wrap connections, weatherproof cases, etc. All of this care will pay off not only in reliability, but also in the service that it will not require later: the mainbox is usually buried in an inaccessible location for protection, making service difficult!

The extra effort put into the design and construction of the main-box will repay itself over and over again during the life of the car and the security system.

FUNCTION

No matter what the level of complexity, all mainboxes function in pretty much the same way. There are certain types of inputs and outputs, and certain ways that the internal circuitry will operate on the input signals to change the outputs. Not every mainbox will have every type of input or output, of course, but a really complex one may have all types, and more than one of some.

Inputs

All security systems have an *arming/disarming* input, an "on-off" control. Simpler mainboxes may just use the power input as their arming control, with arming and disarming being accomplished by interrupting or restoring the power supply. More complex units will probably have a separate input as an arming control. This type of input, like most, will usually be *buffered*. A buffered input is one that has conditioning circuitry to take a weak or fluctuating signal and transform it into a strong, clean signal for the internal circuitry. (A buffered output, on the other hand, is one that can drive an output line without loading or interfering with the internal circuitry.)

With the simple type of arming control, you only have one choice in design: when the power input is low, the system is disarmed, and vice versa. With the separate input, you have a much freer hand with the design of its operation. For instance, you can use either a continuous high or low level to keep the system disarmed, with its complement or absence arming the system. Or you could use a set of frequencies to arm and disarm, or just about any other types of signals that you can think of.

The arming control signal is often passed on through the main-box and out to other, remote modules to reset them (disablers, latching indicators) or switch them down into a low-power-draw standby state (input circuitry, powered sensors). When this tech-nique is used, the outgoing signal must be buffered and have suf-ficient current to drive the other modules.

All mainboxes, of course, have a *trigger* input, and all but the simplest have more than one. The trigger signal may come directly from a sensor, or it may come from the output of an input conditioning module. Either way, the proper signal at the trigger input of the mainbox will cause the mainbox to commence its alarm cycle.

The trigger inputs for all of the systems, mainboxes, and modules in this book are designed to accept a no-connection or high level as their normal state, and a low-level signal, momentary or continuous, as a trigger signal. This point of design will greatly simplify system construction, installation, and operation, since the return side of all sensors and input-conditioning circuitry need only be connected to the frame of a negatively-grounded vehicle in order to complete the loop. Therefore, only a single lead will need to be routed back to the mainbox from most sensors.

The trigger input can be handled in a number of different ways, once received by the mainbox. Most simpler units, with only one input, will immediately use the trigger signal to activate the alarm output. More sophisticated mainboxes will have a second trigger input that accepts the trigger signal and delays for a preset period before passing it along to the alarm output. This would allow the arming control to be placed inside the car. Only the driver's side door would normally be wired to this input, allowing the operator to enter through it and disarm the system before the input delay—the *entry delay*, to be more correct—times out and sounds the alarm. Opening any of the other doors or tripping any of the other sensors would immediately activate the alarm output.

Many systems will have at least a third input, this one designed to accept the outputs of motion and vibration sensors. Their signals would be routed through a *count-delay* circuit before being passed on to the alarm circuitry. (See Chapter 6 for details.)

All three types of inputs can be protected from latch-up conditions caused by a closed sensor by using an *input isolator*. The input isolator keeps a triggered or closed sensor from holding the input line low, thus disabling the other sensors. (Again, see Chapter 6 for details.)

In addition to arming and trigger inputs, mainboxes can be fitted with all types of special control inputs—to change sensitivity, for example, or to switch a subcircuit into or out of operation. The possibilities with special inputs are only limited by your own skill and imagination.

Outputs

A simple security system's mainbox may have only a single output: the alarm output. With all systems in this book, the alarm output is normally low or no-connection, going to a high state to activate the alarm components. The very simplest systems may use a high-current output to drive the alarm devices directly, but the preferred way with all systems is to use a low-current alarm output signal to drive heavier relay devices, or *powerswitches*, that in turn feed power to the siren or bell or whatever. When driving all alarm devices indirectly this way, the alarm output can be limited to sourcing 200 or 300 milliamperes.

There are a number of control and indicator outputs that can be added to the mainbox, the exact types determined by what you want to control or be informed of. Common types of control outputs are, as mentioned, the arming/disarming input signal, or other such on-off signals. A quick look at Chapter 7 will give you an idea of the many types of indicators that can be added to even a simple mainbox.

One important thing to note is that all outputs must be buffered in order to keep them from fouling up the operation of the internal circuitry.

DESIGN

The design of the mainbox is, as mentioned at the beginning of the chapter, the most important part of building a reliable automotive security system. There are a number of basic design principles that will apply no matter what the exact type of mainbox you intend on building for your system.

General Design Principles

The principal point to remember when designing the mainbox is to keep its current draw to an absolute minimum. Since the mainbox is usually the most complicated part of the system, the use of ordinary (by the high standards of this book) design principles could result in a unit that draws too much current. While this particular point is repeated to death throughout this book, its importance cannot be overestimated.

The first step in reducing the current drawn by the mainbox is to use only low-power variants of the ICs in its design. CMOS units are, of course, inherently low-power, but if the design involves any linear ICs, low-power versions (such as the CMOS 7555 for the 555) must be used. Cost is unimportant! Even if the 7555 were 10 times the price of the 555, it would still be a bargain in terms of the current it saves.

A very important current-reducing technique is the use of

current-limiting resistors throughout the mainbox. Inputs, outputs, and internal circuitry alike should all use appropriately-sized resistors to limit their maximum current flow. In some cases, a 1/4- or 1/2-watt unit will be sufficient, as when limiting the base current to a transistor. In other cases—for example, high-current outputs—higher-wattage wirewound units may be needed.

Limiting resistors on the inputs and outputs may, on paper, seem excessive in some cases. You can look at the schematic and see that a particular output will never have to source more than, say, 10 milliamps. Why bother to limit it? Why not? All it will cost is one resistor—a dime or less, even if you use a top-quality metal-film unit, and it could later save you from replacing an entire module or even most of your system because of short-circuit damage.

This example brings up the first—and very, very important—automotive security system design rule: **Never depend on outlying parts of the system to behave!** Each module should be self-sufficient with regard to overcurrent and overvoltage protection, even when such protection is doubly or triply redundant and even when modules are only inches from each other. Protecting the components of your security system is cheap, particularly up against the cost of rebuilding them.

The second general design rule sounds like a contradiction of the first: **simplify everything as much as possible.** This does not mean eliminating necessary components of any kind, but rather revising the design to use a simpler form of a filter, for example, or a fewer-component timing circuit. The logic behind this rule should be obvious: fewer parts means fewer things to go wrong! There are endless ways of achieving a goal using a complex circuit; the trick, in automotive security as well as elsewhere, is to use the simplest circuit that does the job.

The third general design factor derives somewhat from the second: **use innovative design techniques**. If a circuit uses the regular or traditional way to do something, it's probably too complicated or too costly in money or power consumption.

Often, circuits designed to do one job can, with a few minor changes, do a completely different one. For the most part, circuits used in automotive security systems do switching and timing. Switching can be done with relays, transistors, and an endless variety of ICs. Timing functions can be accomplished using (again) transistors, resistor-capacitor junctions, counter ICs, timer ICs, and so on. The idea is that if you look long enough or experiment enough, you'll come up with a better, simpler way to achieve a given function.

The circuits in this book have been designed in accordance with these rules, for the most part, and can be used directly without problems. If you are going to want to do your own design work, you'll need a good familiarity with the major IC families and their quirks. The best place to start is with the various IC family "cookbooks." After that, it's experiment, experiment, experiment.

The fourth and final general design factor comes from Chapter 3: **derate all components.** This is an important step everywhere, but doubly important in such a hardworking component as a mainbox. Derating, you'll remember, is the technique of limiting the load on a component to a fraction of its rated capacity—for example, keeping the current load on a 1-ampere transistor to 500 milliamps or less, or keeping the load on a 1/2-watt resistor to 1/10 of a watt.

If a mainbox—or other complicated module—has its design simplified and its circuitry current-limited and sharply derated, it will be almost unbelievably reliable—which is exactly what you want your automotive security system to be.

Input Design Principles

As mentioned, mainboxes have three types of inputs: trigger, control, and power. All three types need to have three things: bypassing, current-limiting, and off-state stabilization.

Current-limiting, already covered, needs only a quick discussion. Most of a mainbox's inputs are logic-level instead of brute force (with the exception being the power-supply input) and never have more than a few milliamps incoming or outgoing. Therefore, there is no reason not to limit them. Simply insert a resistor into the input line with a value that limits the current to about 150-200 percent of the needed current (for the very small current levels) or to allow an extra 2-3 milliamps (for the larger levels). The current-limiting resistor should be the first component in the input line.

Off-state stabilization simply means to use a pull-up or pull-down resistor to tie the input solidly into its off state. Never depend on the incoming signal or lack of it to hold the input in the proper state. (If this doesn't sound familiar, then you didn't read the first general design principle carefully!)

The value of the pull-up or pull-down resistor will depend upon two things: the amount of current that the input requires to change states, and the speed of the pulse applied (if applicable). The resistor should be large enough to keep parasitic current leakage through it to a minimum, but small enough to keep the input line stable. If the line is, for example, an arming control line, where the incoming control voltage will be either high or low, with no brief pulses or in-between states, then the value of the resistor becomes much less critical. As a general rule of thumb, in these non-critical cases, the value of the resistor should give a pull current of 50-75 percent of the input's nominal input current. For example, if a control input draws one milliamp while being held high, the pull-down resistor should have a pull current of 0.50 to 0.75 milliamp.

The joker comes in when the input may be subject to very brief pulses as inputs. If a pull resistor's value is too small, the pulse may be swamped by the pull current. In these cases, the resistor should be much larger: it should pull about 15-25 percent of the peak input current. Some experimentation may be necessary to make doubly sure that trigger pulses, for example, are always received clearly by the trigger input.

The above two input-conditioning techniques do not, as a rule, apply to the power-supply input. There are some cases where a pull-down resistor may be used to ensure that the device shuts off promptly by rapidly dissipating any charge remaining in the module's capacitors. If the module has more than a small total capacitance, though, this technique will not work; the resistor, in order to speed up the discharging, would have to be of such a small value that the parasitic current it would add during normal operation would be excessive.

Bypassing and filtering applies to all three types of inputs. Bypassing and filtering power-supply inputs has already been covered in Chapter 4, along with the general principles of bypassing and filtering. Bypassing and filtering control and trigger inputs is a touchy, critical business. There are several rules of thumb that make the job easier, but this is one area where there is no substitute for direct hands-on experimentation.

Capacitors used in these applications should be large enough to keep too-brief pulses locked out, but small enough to let the proper pulses through. The smaller the capacitor, the less effect it will have on incoming pulses. The value for filter caps here should range roughly from 0.001 to 1 microfarad.

Zener diodes can be used to protect inputs that may be subjected to overvoltage. The zener should come after the current-limiting resistor and before the bypass or filter capacitors. The rule of thumb is that the zener's voltage should be (for control and trigger inputs) 10 percent over the maximum nominal input voltage. Remember that the zener's wattage should be "five watts for every amp flowing across its terminals," or at least one watt.

Output Design Principles

Outputs, in many ways, are just as finicky as inputs. They can't usually cause problems by themselves, but if they malfunction, they can burn out a poorly designed mainbox or outlying module, or cause the system to act very strangely.

To reiterate: outputs must be conservatively current limited. Integrated circuits should not be used to drive more than a few milliamps, and small transistors should not be pushed past twenty. For heavy output currents (which really should be avoided in the first place), a TO-220 or TO-3 style transistor should be used. Under no circumstances should a mainbox source more than 500 milliamps from any output. (Usually, the only one that will be that high will be the alarm output.)

When current-limiting the alarm output, it's permissible to leave a good-sized leeway between the current limit and the load on the output—up to 100 milliamps. The reason for this is that you're almost sure to want to add just one more alarm device later on, and it would be a hassle to pull the mainbox and upgrade the output. With 100 milliamps of reserve drive current, you should be able to add at least two or three more devices to the system without any modification to the mainbox.

Outputs should have pull-up or pull-down resistors at the very end, just before the outgoing connecting wire, to keep their end of the line tied off properly. Since the input of the module that it's driving should have its own pull resistor, the value of the output's resistor can be very large—up to 10 times the corresponding input's resistor's value.

An important step in output design applies not at the output itself, but farther back into the output circuitry. All parts of the circuitry that determine the output's state—which in some cases would be all of the circuitry in the mainbox—should use all available bypassing techniques to keep the outputs stable, only allowing them to change states on the proper command. (Most ICs have either direct or indirect provisions for bypassing built right in. Refer to the ICs spec sheet if necessary and use the provisions.)

BASIC TYPES

There are endless ways to actually build a mainbox; the exact choice of design will be up to you, your wants, and your particular needs. The very most basic type of mainbox can be represented by a *black box* with four terminals: power, ground, trigger input, and alarm output.

This black box mainbox, shown in Fig. 5-1, would be armed and disarmed by connecting and interrupting the power supply from its power lead. A brief low- or ground-level pulse applied to its trigger input would cause the alarm output to latch into a high state. The alarm output would remain high until the box was at least momentarily disarmed.

That sums up the operation of a basic mainbox. Options such as entry/exit and reset timers, special outputs, special inputs, etc., are up to you.

Relay Mainboxes

The simplest class of mainboxes centers around a DPST-NO relay. The unit shown in Fig. 5-2 is a direct realization of the black box above. When the unit is armed and a trigger impulse is received, the relay will close. One set of contacts takes over for the trigger impulse and keeps the relay latched in the closed state. The other set of contacts closes to source power out to the alarm devices.

Many very inexpensive commercial and homebuilt auto securi-

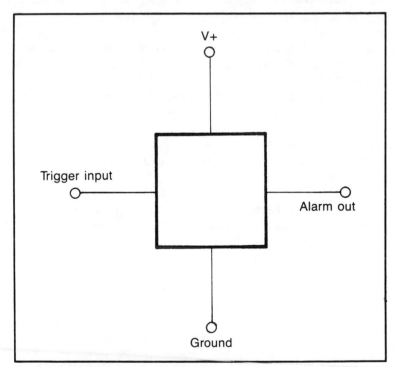

Fig. 5-1. A black box representation of a mainbox.

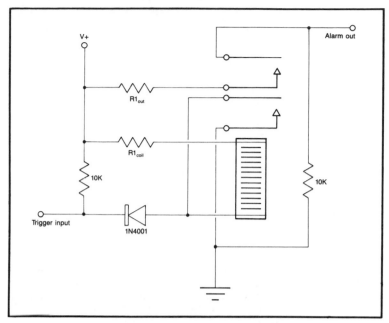

Fig. 5-2. A basic relay-type mainbox. The coil resistor should limit the coil current at a minimum level; the output resistor should be chosen to limit the alarm output current to a safe level.

ty systems use exactly this type of mainbox; in fact, this makes up the entire system for most! It has as its main advantage extreme simplicity and bottom-level cost. The disadvantages are more numerous.

First, its input is a high-current "brute-force" type. Very brief trigger pulses may fail to trigger it into the alarm state. This problem can be alleviated by using a transistor as an input buffer, as shown in Fig. 5-3. The addition of the transistor changes the slow brute-force input into a much faster and more sensitive logic-level one.

The second problem with the basic relay-type mainbox is that it lacks an entry/exit timer, and therefore the arming control must go on the outside of the vehicle. This is one of the most serious flaws of the simpler mainboxes and will be dealt with in a comprehensive manner later on.

The third problem is that it lacks a reset timer, so once the alarm is triggered, it will continue to run either until it is disarmed or the battery runs flat. The big problem with the lack of a reset timer is not really the first drawback—running the battery flat—but the

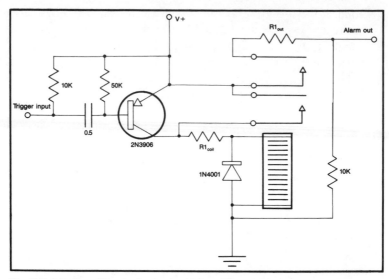

Fig. 5-3. A buffered-input relay-type mainbox. The addition of the transistor gives the mainbox greater sensitivity, allowing it to react to shorter trigger pulses. The coil and output limiting resistors should be chosen to limit the respective currents to safe levels.

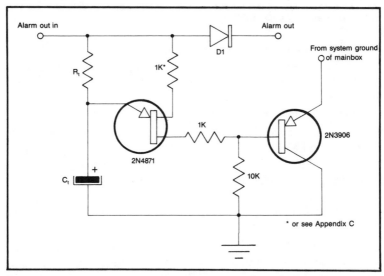

Fig. 5-4. The unijunction reset timer can be used with any of the simple mainboxes (Figs. 5-2, 5-3, 5-6, 5-7) or added to an existing commercial system that lacks a reset. The alarm output of the mainbox is fed to the ALARM OUT IN terminal and the ALARM OUT terminal is used as the new alarm output. The ground connection of the mainbox should be routed through the PNP transistor. Diode D1 must have an I_f sufficient to handle the alarm output current.

second. If the unit isn't reset, and quickly, by the owner, it's likely to be reset by an annoyed neighbor. If that means damaging the car to do it, that's just tough. Since it's so easy to add a reset timer, there's really no reason not to.

The unijunction type reset timer is quite simple to add to a basic relay-type mainbox. The circuit still functions in the same way, with one exception. When the relay closes, the alarm output also supplies power to a simple unijunction transistor circuit (Fig. 5-4). This circuit's RC junction charges up the uni's trigger point, and the uni then fires, dumping the capacitor's charge and momentarily interrupting power to the relay.

The unijunction type reset timer is the simplest, and does not draw any standby power. However, the 555-type reset timer, shown in Fig. 5-5, gives a number of advantages at once.

First, you get a buffered, logic-level input, along with a precise, programmable timing interval, and a more flexible system in general. The disadvantage is that it draws an appreciable amount of standby current. The advantage of the simple relay type over all other types is that in its simplest form, it draws zero power while on standby—which can be an overriding factor for some systems.

Relays, as the core of a mainbox, are not recommended for any but the simplest low-budget installations.

Discrete-Component Mainboxes

The relay in the simplest types of mainboxes can be replaced by discrete components. The most common replacements are the thyristor "semiconductor relays:" the SCR and the triac.

These three-terminal semiconductor devices can be set up so that a brief pulse at their gate terminal will latch them into conducting. The SCR, shown as the heart of the mainbox in Fig. 5-6, can only be triggered by a high pulse; the triac, shown in Fig. 5-7, can be triggered by either a high or low pulse. For this reason, the triac is more suitable for use as the core of an automotive security system's mainbox. It may be difficult to find small, TO-92-cased sensitive-gate triacs, though, and the larger variety can be excessive in its current consumption.

The only critical part of the thyristor type mainbox is the value of the thyristor's hold-on resistor (R_{hold}). It should be as high as possible to limit parasitic current, but low enough to ensure that the thyristor is solidly latched on.

The unijunction reset timer can be added to the thyristor-type mainbox in the same way that it is added to the relay type.

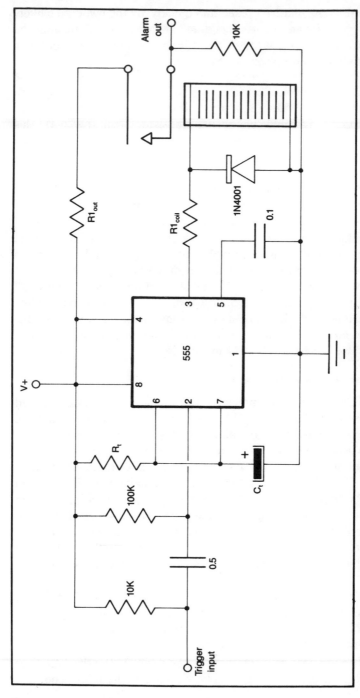

Fig. 5-5. A relay-type mainbox with a 555 reset timer. The use of the 555 gives both a buffered input and a precise reset interval. See Appendix B for timing information. A low-power 555 variant, such as the L555, is recommended here.

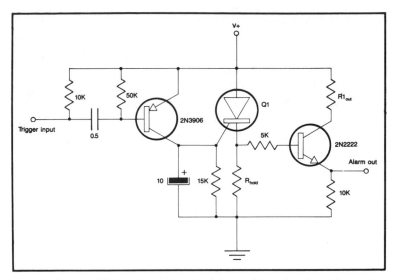

Fig. 5-6. A basic SCR-type mainbox. A trigger pulse at the trigger input trips the SCR into conduction via the PNP transistor. Q1 is any TO-92-cased, sensitive-gate SCR. The SCR's hold-on resistor R_{hold} must have sufficient pull to hold the SCR in its latched state even when V+ drops to about 80 percent of its full value.

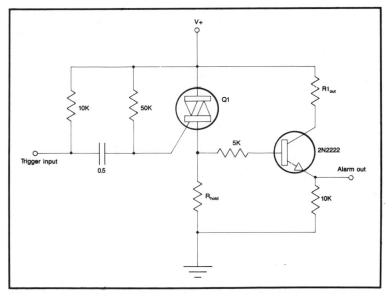

Fig. 5-7. A basic triac-type mainbox. This type is superior to the SCR type due to its lower component count. Again, the resistor R_{hold} should be selected to keep the triac latched on with V+ as low as 80 percent. Q1 is any sensitive-gate triac.

Integrated-Circuit Mainboxes

Once integrated circuits come into your system design, the system will do more things more easily and more reliably—which of course illustrates the basic value of ICs.

The simplest IC mainbox design uses the cheap and ubiquitous CMOS 4001 chip (Fig. 5-8). It has an extremely low-current but precise trigger input, a reset timer, and—best of all—extraordinarily low current draw. In the standby mode, this mainbox draws less than 3 microamperes, and in the alarm state, less than 2 milliamps—an outstanding set of figures.

In this design, two of the four NOR gates are cross-coupled into a simple set-reset flip-flop, with the other two acting as input and output buffers. The timing period is determined by the RC network according to the following formula:

$$t = 0.693R_tC_t$$

The delay time, t, is in seconds, R_t is the timing resistance in megohms, and C_t is the timing capacitance in microfarads. Due to the extremely high input impedance of CMOS (approximately 10^{12} ohms), the timing components can have very large values for long time periods. The only limiting factor will be the leakage of the capacitor—and if a high-quality, high WVdc solid tantalum unit is used, the leakage will be very low. Timing periods of thirty minutes or more can be achieved with this circuit. Since CMOS outputs cannot source more than a few milliamps, a driver, such as the transistor shown in Fig. 5-8, must be used.

What's interesting about the 4001-type mainbox is that a block diagram of its circuitry very closely resembles that of a monolithic IC timer such as the 555. In fact, the 555 and the few outboard components that it requires are more flexible and easier to use than the 4001! With the exception of power consumption (even low-power versions of the 555 draw close to a milliamp on standby), the monolithic timer makes a better choice. Add in the fact that the 4001 and 555 are about the same price, with the low-power versions somewhat higher, and there isn't any reason to use anything else!

In fact, the 555 and its numerous derivatives, the 556 dual timer, the 558 quad timer, the 7555 and 7556 CMOS units, and the L555 and L556 low-power monolithic variations, make up such a useful, flexible group of chips that their use is widespread throughout this book. An entire appendix has been devoted to the specifics of their use, so if you're not familiar with their operation, refer to Appendix B before continuing.

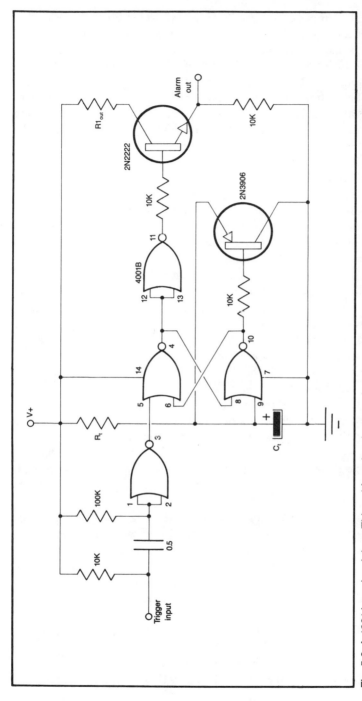

Fig. 5-8. A 4001-based mainbox. This unit's main advantage is an extremely low standby current draw, as well as incorporating a reset timer. Be certain to use a B-series IC, not an A-series. See text for timing information.

The simplest 555-based mainbox shown in Fig. 5-9 uses a transistor as an alarm output buffer, in accordance with the general design rules. The 555 can source or sink about 300 milliamps directly, but by isolating it from heavy current draw, many problems can be eliminated before they start.

The above four types of mainbox design each have their advantages and disadvantages, but all are seriously compromised by one common factor: their arming controls must be on the outside of the vehicle, and thus outside the protection area of the security system. For the very simplest applications, this won't be too big of a problem, but for high-risk vehicles and those that can't be marred by a keyswitch on the outside, another solution must be found.

The solution, of course, is to put the arming control on the inside of the vehicle, which raises a problem: how do you arm and disarm the system without tripping the alarm? The solution is to use an entry/exit delay timer.

An exit delay timer circuit delays the actual arming of the system to allow you time to arm the system, get out, and shut the door behind you. After its delay period times out, the system is allowed to arm normally.

The entry delay timer delays triggering of the system to allow you to enter—usually through the driver's side door only—and disarm the system. If the system is not disarmed before the timer runs out, the system will go into the alarm state.

The mainbox shown in Fig. 5-10 is a basic building-block design incorporating an entry/exit delay and a reset timer. It is constructed around two ICs, a 555 and a 556. It is this design that should be used as the core for all more complex designs, and those that use the input-conditioning circuitry and other high-performance add-ons. Its importance warrants a fairly thorough discussion of its operation.

The 555, wired as a half-astable, acts as the exit delay. (Although it functions as a monostable, it is actually an astable that never completes the second half of its cycle, hence, half-astable.) Upon power-up, its output goes high, holding the rest of the system off, until it times out. On timeout, it allows the remainder of the system to come up—which should be after you are out of the vehicle and the doors, etc., are shut.

This mainbox has two trigger inputs, one direct and one delayed. The delayed input, which should be connected only to the driver's side door sensor (or its functional equivalent, in another type of vehicle), goes to the entry timer. The entry timer, which is the first half

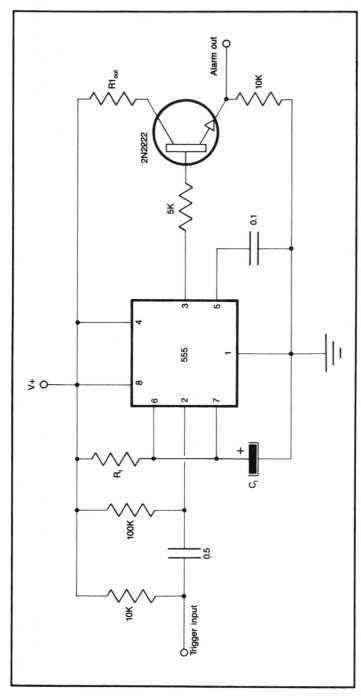

Fig. 5-9. A basic 555-based mainbox. The output transistor is required to keep the current load low on the 555's output. The use of a low-power 555 variant is recommended.

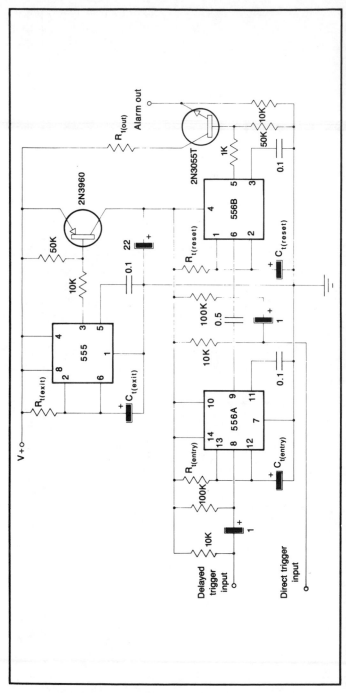

Fig. 5-10. The building-block mainbox. This unit has entry, exit, and reset timers, direct and delayed trigger inputs, and a buffered output. This is the design to use for all sophisticated systems—with the addition of the deadman control, it becomes a very formidable core for a topnotch system. Low-power 555 and 556 variants are required.

of the 556, will go through its timing cycle, its output going high and then low after it times out; if the system has not been disarmed by that point, the negative-going edge of the pulse will trip the reset timer into operation.

The direct trigger input acts in the same manner, except that it bypasses the entry timer and immediately trips the reset timer.

The second half of the 556 is used as the reset or output timer. When it is triggered, either by a direct input or from the output of the entry timer, its resulting high output in turn drives the alarm output high. When its timing cycle is complete, the alarm output will drop low, and the system will be reset, ready for the next trigger impulse.

The actual delay periods used for the entry, exit, and reset timers are of course variable and can be set to any length that suits your needs. There are recommended ranges, however.

The exit delay timer can be set from 30 to 90 seconds, depending on how long it will take you to get your things together and get out. Leaving this period long is usually permissible, since it is doubtful that a thief will be able to break into the car before you are out of sight. The extra time will come in handy for those times when you have passengers or a large number of packages to gather up.

The entry delay timer can be set from 5 to 20 seconds. This setting is more critical, since it determines the amount of time a thief would have inside the car to tamper with the arming control. It should be as short as possible, allowing you just enough time to open the door, toss in your coat or briefcase or packages, get in, and disarm the system, with a little leeway to allow fumbling around.

The reset timing period can be from 1 to 10 minutes. If you use only a silent alarm pager, which requires only a short trigger pulse, this period can be set even shorter—a few seconds or so. In most cases, though, you will want the alarm to sound for a period long enough to attract attention, but short enough to keep it from irritating neighbors and police. A good all-around range is from 3 to 5 minutes. Recall from Chapter 2 that many communities have noise laws that limit such reset times: keep your system within the law. If your system lacks a reset or its reset period is too long, an obliging passerby may reset the system for you—with a sledgehammer!

From these five mainbox designs, you should be able to choose one that will work well for your needs, or at least understand how to modify one of them so that it does. Remember that a mainbox is only the central part of a security system, and that there are endless other modules and options that can enhance its operation. The possibilities for internal options are below; external options will be found in the next three chapters.

OPTIONS AND MODIFICATIONS

There are several options that can be added to the basic mainbox. The first, the *deadman arming control* of Fig. 5-11, is the trickiest and is universally recommended. Despite its simplicity, it is one of the single most effective add-ons you can have.

As its name implies, the deadman control is one that functions only when "dead," or disconnected. As long as its input is held high, the system is disarmed. When its input drops low, the system will commence arming. The trick here is that the arming control, be it keyswitch, keypad, or whatever, will work in exactly the opposite manner that would be expected. When the control is off, the system is on. When the control is on, then, the system will be off! The up-

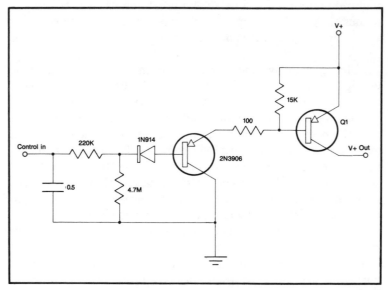

Fig. 5-11. A very effective addition to any system: the deadman arming control. When the CONTROL IN terminal is held high by the arming switch or keypad output, the V+ OUT terminal will be off. When the CONTROL IN terminal drops low or is disconnected, the V+ OUT terminal will go high. Q1 must have sufficient current capability handle the draw of the mainbox and whatever other circuits draw power through it. This circuit is characterized for 12-volt use; if used with another voltage, the 220K and 4.7M resistors must be adjusted in proportion. In the off state, the circuit draws about 0.1 milliamp.

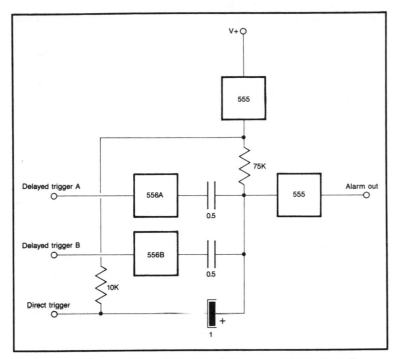

Fig. 5-12. Multiple entry delays. Using Fig. 5-10 as a model, this block diagram illustrates how a second 555 is used for the reset timer, allowing you to use both halves of the 556 as entry timers. The first timer, connected to the driver's side door, should delay for the normal entry period; the second, connected to the passenger door(s), should give extra time to allow passengers to get in before you do. See text for limitations on its use.

shot is that a thief can break into the vehicle and destroy the arming control—smash it, rip it out, cut its wires—and the system will be unaffected; it will keep right on counting down towards the alarm state. To a large extent, too, the deadman control can cover for your own mistakes. If you leave the system disarmed and a thief tries to "disarm" it, he'll wind up arming it instead!

Multiple entry delays are another possibility. With a single entry delay, you have to jump in, disarm the systems, and then get out and go around to open the door for your date or wife (assuming you're basically courteous in the first place). As Fig. 5-12 shows, by using a second 555 for the reset timer, you can use both halves of the 556 as input delay timers. The first would be left the same, and the driver's side door connected to it. The second would have a somewhat longer delay and would be connected to the passenger door. This would give you time to open the door for your passenger and go around to your door and get in before disarming the system normally.

The use of a multiple entry delay in this manner compromises the security of your system somewhat, since a thief coming in via the passenger door would have that much longer to wreak havoc. It's up to you to choose what's more important in your own case, courtesy or security.

The second entry delay could have other uses as well, such as the input line of a sensitive motion or vibration sensor. That way, you would have an extra 5 seconds or so of jiggling and shaking the car as you unlock it, without accidental triggering of the alarm.

Multiple outputs are another useful addition to a mainbox. Indicator outputs will be covered in Chapter 7.

One type of auxiliary output that has already been mentioned is an extension of the arming control (Fig. 5-13). Here the signal from the arming input or deadman control output is buffered, amplified, and sent out to outlying modules to reset them or to switch them into low-power-draw off states. This same type of output could be used to pick up other of the mainbox's internal signals and pass them on to the outside parts of the system. Whatever the signal or its use, a buffer should be used so that the original signal remains

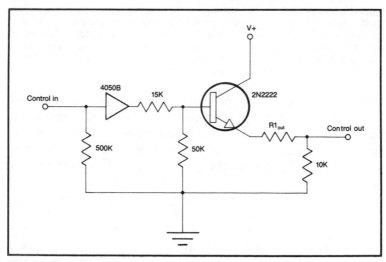

Fig. 5-13. The arming-control extension. The CONTROL IN terminal should be connected to the V+ bus of the mainbox. When it goes high (i.e., the system is armed) the CONTROL OUT terminal will also go high. The outgoing signal can be used to reset the switch on and off outlying modules. By replacing the 4050 with a 4049 and tying the 500K resistor to V+, the operation can be reversed (i.e., the output will be high when the system is disarmed.)

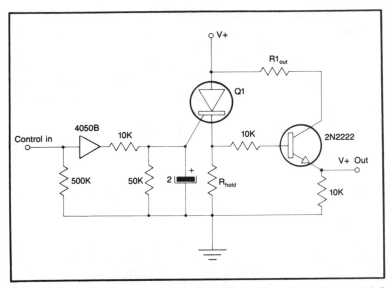

Fig. 5-14. The latching output extension. Identical to Fig. 5-13 except that a brief high pulse on the input will latch the output high. The V+ supply should come from a switched portion of the mainbox, so that the output will unlatch when the system is disarmed. The 4050 to 4049 change described in Fig. 5-13 can also be used here. Q1 is any sensitive-gate SCR.

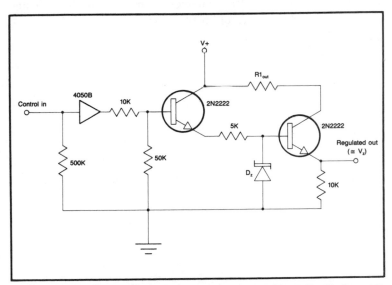

Fig. 5-15. The regulated output extension. Identical to Fig. 5-13 with the addition of a transistor-zener bridge on the output to give a regulated output voltage. The output voltage will be approximately equal to V_z. This circuit, with a 5-volt zener for D_z, would be ideal to drive the flashing LED of Chapter 7.

103

unaffected. The CMOS 4049 and 4050 ICs are good choices for the first stage of such buffers, due to the high input impedance of CMOS circuitry. If more current is needed, the CMOS buffer can be used to drive an output transistor, and if the output is to latch on, the buffer chip can drive a sensitive-gate SCR (Fig. 5-14). If the latter is used, make sure that the SCR's hold-on resistor (R_{hold}) has a value that is low enough to keep the SCR latched on.

The same output circuit could be used as a switched power-supply output. Such an output would be controlled by the arming input, whether direct or deadman, and be able to switch its output power on or off accordingly. The output power could then be used for powered sensors, outlying modules, and the like. Be certain that the final stage of the output is capable of handling the current demand of the items it powers.

The switched power supply output can be made into a regulated output by adding a transistor-zener bridge to the output of the circuit in Fig. 5-13; the result would be Fig. 5-15. This circuit can be used to supply switched, regulated power to outlying modules and powered sensors.

There are a number of ways to modify and decode the trigger inputs for greater sensitivity, fewer falses, and better operation overall. The circuitry involved will often be installed inside the main-box case, but will be covered in the next chapter.

6

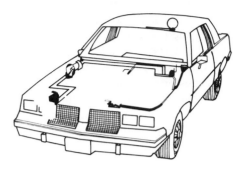

Sensors and Input Conditioning

S ENSORS ARE THE NERVE ENDS OF AN AUTOMOTIVE SECURITY system. They are the devices that actually sense tampering and unauthorized entry. They can take any of hundreds of forms, from simple pinswitches to complex sonar listening devices, and anything else in between.

Sensors alone can't do very much, obviously, and even a sensor and a mainbox together only make up half a system; all sensors need at least an elementary form of input conditioning. Input conditioning can range from a pull-up or pull-down resistor on the trigger input to a complex count-delay circuit. In one form or another, input conditioning's purpose is to assist or translate the sensor's signal into a form that the mainbox can use more efficiently or reliably.

SENSOR PRINCIPLES

Basically, a sensor is any mechanical or electronic device that transmits a signal to the mainbox when it detects vibration, motion of the vehicle, the opening of a door or hood, or any other "happening" that indicates tampering. A sensor can be bought, built, or modified to detect virtually any phenomenon.

The most basic type of sensor is a normally-closed pushbutton switch that is held in the open position by a closed door, hood, or hatch lid. When the door or whatever is opened, the switch will close and pass a trigger signal along to the mainbox, either directly or via input conditioning circuitry.

The second common type of sensor is the motion or vibration sensing type. These units use a fixed contact pad and a moving contact on a spring arm. The gap between the two can be adjusted—the smaller the gap, the less shock force required to close it. The motion sensor is fairly large, with a long, soft spring arm, and the vibration sensor is smaller, with a shorter, stiffer spring arm. The motion sensor will respond primarily to slow, long-period oscillations of the vehicle, while the vibration sensor will respond primarily to short, sharp shocks. The two types are usually used in conjunction for maximum coverage.

Beyond these two basic types of sensors, anything is possible. The largest class of the more complex sensors are the listening types; they listen for a given sound or frequency from subaudio to supra-audio. The subaudio range could be to listen for creaking of the frame or body, for example, and the supra-audio could be used to listen for the noise of breaking glass or scraping of metal. The audio range could be used to listen for any sound over a certain level inside the car. Another type of sensor would look for the presence or absence of a voltage at a given point in the electrical system, or a spike in the main electrical system. The possibilities are numerous.

All of the security systems in this book are designed to accept a high level or a no-connection as their normal trigger-input state, and a low level—continuous or mementary—as a trigger signal. This design is virtually universal with off-the-shelf security equipment as well.

Remember that in Chapter 2 it was mentioned that one of the most common failings of commercial automotive security systems was an overdependence on a single type of sensing. Don't make this mistake with your system. *No security system should be dependent on a single type of sensor or sensing!* The principle of redundant and overlapping sensing is one of the most important to remember when designing a system's sensor array. With redundant sensing, even if a thief manages to find and defeat a single sensor—or even several—one or more will still be waiting to trip him up.

Sensor Types

Even if you discount the oddball, single-use types of sensors, there are still dozens of designs available. In most cases, for each single type of sensing, there will be several different designs of sensor. Once you have chosen your basic system design parameters, you can pick through this section and choose the exact sensor designs that meet your needs.

There are two basic classes of sensor: remote and direct.

Remote Sensors

Remote sensors are the types of sensing units that cover all or most of the vehicle from a single point. They should not be used alone—even two types of remote sensors together are not an acceptable sensor array by themselves. The primary use of remote sensors is to detect tampering and unauthorized entry attempts, as opposed to direct sensors which generally detect entry at a specific point. There are two subclasses of remote sensors, mechanical and electronic.

Mechanical remote sensors tend to be of the motion and vibration type, although there are probably others. Motion sensors, as mentioned in Chapter 2, tend to be the most overrated and over-gimmicked part of many systems. Once a week, like clockwork, someone comes out with a new and improved design. There is nothing wrong with the old rectangular aluminum can type. It is cheap, widely adjustable, sensitive, and easy to use. It should always be used with a count-delay input-conditioning circuit (see below) in all but the simplest systems. There are almost no systems that would be better without it. A motion sensor can detect such a wide variety of theft- and tampering-type phenomena that it can easily become the backbone of any system's sensor array.

The motion sensor can be used in another way as well. A normally-set motion sensor should not be omitted, but a second one, set for very large shocks and used without a count-delay, could be used as a collision sensor, immediately tripping the alarm if someone bumps into your vehicle with theirs—eliminating hit-and-runs.

The vibration sensor tends also to be of a single type. It is usually a small plastic rectangle designed primarily for building use. It is, like the motion sensor, a cheap, sensitive, flexible type of sensor. Both types are illustrated in Fig. 6-1. The differences between the vibration and motion sensors can be used to the great advantage of the system designer: instead of trying to make one sensor detect the whole range of motion and vibration, the two can be used to backstop each other, each one covering one end of the spectrum. If commercial systems would use this simple trick, much of their ineffectiveness would be eliminated.

The electronic types of remote sensors are more diverse and

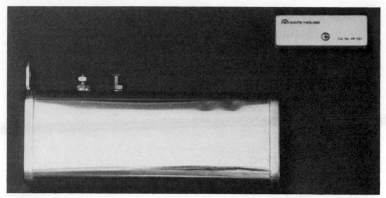

Fig. 6-1. The large aluminum-can type motion sensor, when backed up by the proper input-conditioning circuitry, is still the best way to sense vehicle movement. The smaller vibration sensor is ideal for sensing the short, sharp shocks that come with a forcible entry attempt. These are both Radio Shack units.

numerous, and only limited in type by the designer's imagination. There are two basic types of electronic remote sensor: listeners and voltage-spike monitors.

The listeners, as mentioned above, can be used to listen for any type of noise. No specific designs for this type of sensor are presented here, for several reasons. First, they are difficult to adjust and use properly, and second, there are so many variations in design that to show even a representative sample would be prohibitive in terms of space. If you are interested, there are a few basics that can help you design your own.

First, the actual pickup can be either a microphone or a piezoelectric crystal. The former is used for subaudio and audio frequencies, and the latter is used primarily for supra-audio pickup. Both types are mounted near where the noise would originate, such as on the transmission hump at the firewall to pick up door noises. The circuit design would consist of an amplification stage with adjustable gain, a notch or bandpass filter, likewise adjustable, and an output stage. A switchable power supply, controlled by the arming control of the mainbox, should be used, and care should be taken that the sensor turns on and off cleanly, with no false signals.

The other common type of electronic remote sensor is an all-electrical-system voltage spike monitor. This is the most common type of sensor found on very inexpensive commercial systems. It watches for a voltage spike on the main portion of the electrical system; in theory, the opening of a door or the activation of any electrical component will cause spike that will trip the alarm. In practice, the spike generated may be either too weak to trip the alarm or may be caused by a loose connection or other spurious source. The main reason that this type of sensor is so common is that it is cheap and simple to produce and simple for an inexperienced installer to connect. To put it bluntly, it has no place in any security system that's in a car you care about. It is only discussed here to make this book's coverage complete.

There is a third type of remote sensing that will only guard the interior of the vehicle against unauthorized entry: the ultrasonic sonar unit. It cannot be used with open or convertible body styles, of course, but it may have use in almost any other type of vehicle. It would be best in a large, long body such as that on a station wagon, van, or bus where direct sensors may not be feasible or give adequate protection. Any movement within its sweep area will trip the alarm. Once again, no specific design information will be presented here because of the extreme complexity of ultrasonic circuit design and adjustment. There are several commercial security systems available that center around an ultrasonic sensor, and it would be easier to purchase one and modify it to act as a sensor for your system than it would be for any but an experienced high-frequency circuit designer to build one from scratch. (I had intended on presenting modification information for Heathkit's version, since it was a kit and easily available, but they declined to furnish the needed information.)

Direct Sensors

Direct sensors, as opposed to remote sensors, detect a phenomenon at a specific point instead of over a large area. They only cover one door, for example, or one hatch, or one point of the electrical system. Unlike the remote sensors, their sensitivity can be made much higher without fear of falsing. Like remote sensors, direct sensors can be divided into mechanical and electronic types.

The simplest and most universal type of mechanical direct sensor is the SPST-NO pushbutton switch, used to detect an open door, hood, or trunk/hatch, or the removal of a spare tire, gas can, or other removable item. Mechanically, it can take any form. For doors, the best type of switch is the existing courtesy-light switch. If your car doesn't have a courtesy-light switch on both or all doors, you can probably pick up duplicates of the driver's door unit at the dealer or a wrecking yard. Alternately, for universal use, the all-metal General Motors design can be used. They were used on nearly all GM products from the mid-seventies on, and can be obtained from either GM dealers or wrecking yards.

For doors with larger-than-usual gaps and for hoods and trunk lids, there are special switches designed specifically for such use called pinswitches (Fig. 6-2). They are available in standard and extra-long plunger lengths, about 1/2 inch and 1 inch long respectively. They can be found at Radio Shack and other electronics and auto parts stores. Care should be used in mounting the pinswitch so that neither people nor cargo can get snagged on its plunger.

Since both the courtesy-light and pinswitch types use their cases and in turn the body of the car for their ground return, they should be mounted firmly in a metal surface, or have a separate ground lead attached. Many cars use plastic panels and may have isolated metal subframes, so take care to make sure that your sensor has a solid ground. (This isn't as silly as it sounds. When the first Corvettes rolled off the assembly line, they wouldn't start and none of the electricals worked because the engineers failed to consider the fact that fiberglass wasn't conductive.)

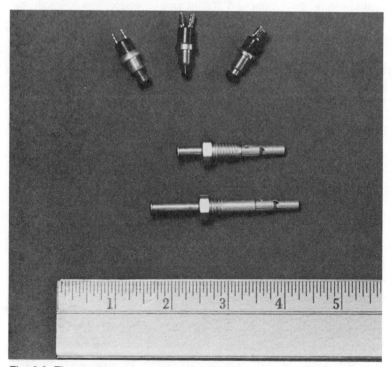

Fig. 6-2. The regular and extra-length pinswitches, bottom, are designed for use with hoods, trunks, hatches, gas-cap doors, and the like. The pushbuttons above are merely representative of some of the types available.

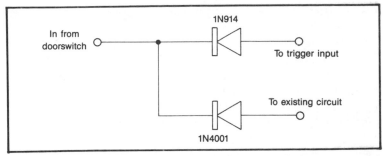

Fig. 6-3. This isolator should be used whenever a courtesy-light switch is used as a sensor. The two diodes prevent signals from cross-feeding and causing problems between the light or buzzer circuit and the security system. A 1N914 or similar diode is adequate for the security system line, but the other line's diode should have sufficient current capacity to handle its load. The 1N4001 shown can handle about 1 amp.

If a sensor switch serves another function, such as control of the courtesy lights or key-in-ignition buzzer, as well as acting as a sensor, the two outgoing lines should be isolated from each other with diodes, as shown in Fig. 6-3, to prevent ghost signals from feeding back and forth.

There are many electronic direct-sensor designs, most of which are solid-state replacements for the pinswitch. There are cases where a mechanical switch may not work, for technical or even esthetic

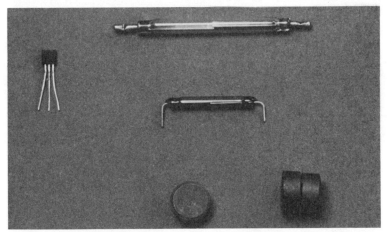

Fig. 6-4. Magnetic sensing elements. The reed switches are cheaper, but they are fragile and not as sensitive as the solid-state Hall-effect sensor at left; however, they draw no standby current. Button magnets of the type below the switches are the most suitable for automotive security use, due to their small size; high-gauss Alnico V types may be needed if the gap is very wide or if other sensitivity problems crop up.

reasons. In these cases, an infrared or magnetic sensor can be used instead.

The magnetic sensor can be either a reed-switch or Hall-effect sensor (Fig. 6-4). Both types work in essentially the same way. As Fig. 6-5 shows, a magnet, either hidden or visible, is mounted to the door, hood, or hatch lid, and the sensor itself is mounted opposite the magnet on the doorframe. The Hall-effect sensor (Fig. 6-6) is a solid-state realization of the fragile and less sensitive reed switch (Fig. 6-7). It is available from most good electronics supply houses, including Radio Shack.

Mountain West Security's catalog lists a simple reed switch with pop-in mounting designed specifically for steel doors, said to be good for up to a 1-inch gap. You might consider using a switch like that rather than designing your own mounting system.

The IR sensor (Fig. 6-8) is similar, but can be made even less

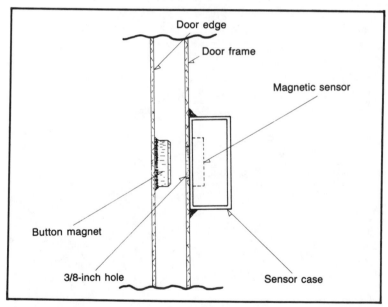

Fig. 6-5. Mounting magnetic sensors. The sensor package should go on the door or hatch frame, and the magnet on the door or hatch. Be sure to mount the whole assembly at a point far from the hinges, so that even the slightest opening of the door or hatch will break the sensor/magnet field. Any type of strong adhesive can be used to mount the two parts to the body; the magnet can be painted body color to minimize obtrusiveness. The hole through the panel for the sensor must be large enough not to interrupt the magnet's field. The 3/8-inch hole shown should be large enough for most purposes, but for less-sensitive switches or larger gaps, a larger hole—up to 3/4-inch—might be needed.

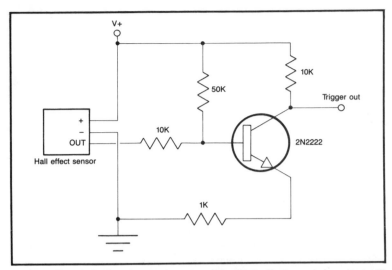

Fig. 6-6. The Hall-effect magnetic sensor. The Hall-effect sensor's output will remain low as long as a magnetic field of proper polarity is applied to its face. Follow the orientation requirements that come with the particular sensor IC you use. As long as the output is low, the output of the transistor will remain high; when the magnetic field is broken, the transistor will drop low and trigger the alarm. This circuit has a fairly high current draw when powered from 12 volts, so a regulated and switched 5 volt supply might be added to the mainbox to power these sensors and bring the current down.

obtrusive than the magnetic type. An infrared-emitting LED goes on one side of the door gap, and an infrared-sensitive photodiode or phototransistor makes up the sensor on the other side (Fig. 6-9). Alternately, the transmitter and receiver can be placed side-by-side on the doorframe, and a reflective patch (mylar, aluminum foil) on the door will bounce the IR light from the LED to the phototransistor (Fig. 6-10). The disadvantage of the IR type is its fairly high current draw: it's difficult to get the LED to transmit sufficient light with less than the ten milliamps of drive current. A pulsed drive could be used to minimize draw. The advantage of the IR type sensor is that it can be made extremely inconspicuous, which could be an overriding factor when installing a system in a fine or classic car.

The other common type of direct electronic sensor is the spot voltage monitor. Instead of the broad coverage given by the main-electrical-system type, the spot voltage monitor watches for the presence or absence of a voltage at a specific point in the electrical system. Uses for the voltage-seeking type (Fig. 6-11A) would include the brake lights, backup lights, or ignition switch. Even if a thief were able to defeat all of the sensors up to that point, he would trip

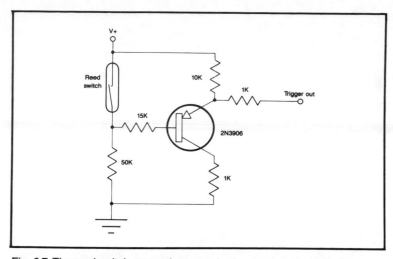

Fig. 6-7. The reed-switch magnetic sensor is simpler than the Hall-effect type, and draws less standby current, although it is more fragile. Its function is very similar to the Hall-effect sensor, except that as long as the switch is held closed by the magnet, it holds the transistor's base high, and in turn, the transistor's output high; when the magnet is moved away, the transistor's base and output drop low.

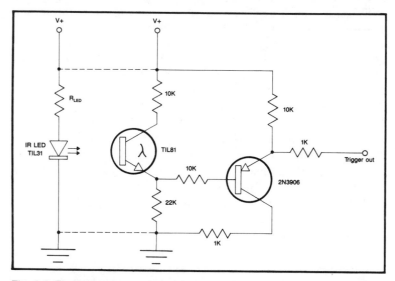

Fig. 6-8. The infrared sensor is probably the least obtrusive way to protect a door. The basic circuit is simple: the LED and its resistor can be part of the sensor circuit or separate, depending on which type of mounting is used. A high-output IR LED such as the TIL31 or XC-880 should be used. (Although almost any IR LED and phototransistor can be used, the TIL31 and TIL81 shown are a matched set, both mechanically and electrically.)

114

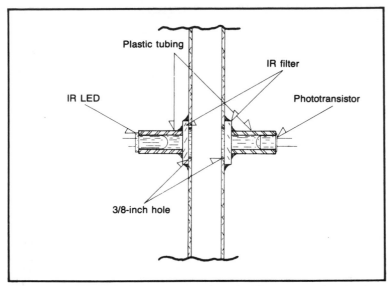

Fig. 6-9. The across-the-gap mounting of an IR LED sensor is the simplest, but It requires running wiring into the door or hatch itself. Note that IR filter material (translucent red plastic, like that used for LED contrast filters, will do, but real IR-transparent material should be used if you can find it) is used on both sides of the gap to limit ambient light interference.

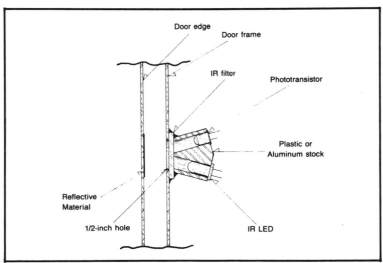

Fig. 6-10. The bounced-light mounting of the IR LED is trickier to align and to make function properly, but it only requires routing wiring to the door jamb, and not into the door or hatch itself. The sensor and emitter are mounted at a 30 degree angle in a block of plastic or other workable material and optically joined by a reflective patch of mylar, aluminum, or stainless steel on the door itself. Very tricky to adjust, but worth it in terms of its low level of obtrusiveness.

115

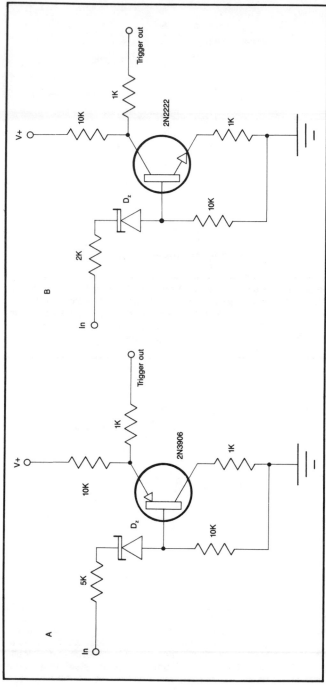

Fig. 6-11. Spot-voltage monitors. These circuits can be used to look for the presence or absence of a voltage at a point where it would indicate tampering. (A) the voltage-absence sensor's output will remain high as long as its input voltage remains higher than V_z; V_z should be about 60-75 percent of V+. (B) The voltage-presence sensor's output will remain as high as its input voltage remains lower than V_z; V_z should be about 25-30 percent of V+. These circuit are very easy to add a system and very effective backup sensing devices.

the alarm when he stepped on the brake pedal or put the transmission into reverse or turned the ignition on. The complementary type that looks for the absence of a voltage (Fig. 6-11B) could be used to doubly protect the vehicle's main battery, if the system is equipped with a backup power supply, by tripping the alarm if the apparent main battery voltage dropped to zero.

INPUT CONDITIONING

In between the sensor, be it remote or direct, and the trigger input of the mainbox, there must be some form of input conditioning. This conditioning can range from a single pull-up resistor to a complex translation circuit. The addition of the simpler forms is mandatory, and the inclusion of the more complex types can improve an already good system immeasurably.

Basics

All trigger inputs must be tied into their normal high state at the mainbox itself. The usual technique is a single or multiple pull-up resistor with sufficient pull current to hold the line high against too-brief false trigger pulses.

If the input is exposed to a large number of false pulses, or to doubly protect against infrequent ones, a filter capacitor can be added between the input and V+. The value should be between 0.01

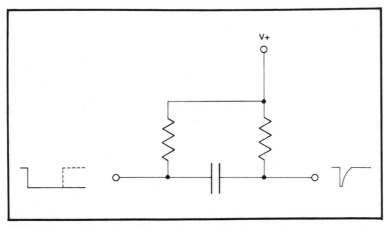

Fig. 6-12. The differentiator will isolate an input line from the trigger input, preventing latch-up conditions. When a falling edge (of either a permanent drop or of a pulse) arrives at the input of the differentiator, the RC network turns it into a brief negative pulse. See text for data on determining resistor and capacitor values.

and 1 μF, with the larger values reserved for worst-case situations.

An excellent addition to trigger inputs is a differentiator, a special type of RC network, shown in Fig. 6-12. A series capacitor and two pull-up resistors act to let pulses through almost unaffected, and to turn the falling edge of a voltage drop into a pulse. A sensor left in a closed position—such as when a thief pops the trunk and is scared off by the alarm, leaving the trunk open—will not continually retrigger the alarm. If the mainbox is equipped with a reset timer, the alarm will reset after the normal time period and not return to the alarm state. The current drawn by the input and the sensor will not become excessive, since they are effectively isolated from each other. All in all, a differentiator is a worthwhile addition to both mainboxes and the input of the more complex input conditioning circuits.

The value of the capacitor will depend upon the strength of the pulse that is required by the mainbox. Relay-types require a fairly hefty trigger pulse, and so will need a fairly large capacitor—on the order of 10 μF—to ensure that sufficient current gets through. Transistor and IC inputs require far less current for triggering, and so a much smaller capacitor—on the order of 1 μF—can be used. If a polarized type of capacitor is used, the positive terminal should be on the inner (electronics module) side, with the negative terminal towards the input line.

The values of the pull-up resistors also vary. The outermost resistor must usually be smaller in value than the innermost one. The outer resistor is responsible for holding the input line high and ensuring that when the trigger pulse comes, it will give a sharp enough drop to pass through the capacitor. The inner resistor is responsible for holding the circuitry's input high to receive the trigger pulse after it passes through the capacitor. The actual values of the resistors should be as high as possible to minimize parasitic current leakage through them. For a relay-type mainbox, the outer resistor should be around 3-5K, and the inner, around 10K. For solid-state inputs, the resistors can be about 10K and 100K, respectively.

There may be cases, particularly when integrating off-the-shelf components into your system, when the trigger signal may not be of the proper polarity, have sufficient level, or may just have the wrong protocol. In these cases, translation circuitry like that shown in Chapter 9 must be used. It is best to avoid the use of such bandaids when possible by modifying or redesigning the parts of the system to work together directly.

Input Isolation

The great problem with the differentiator, although it prevents endless retriggering of the system, is that one closed sensor on that input line disables all of the rest. If, as in the above example, the trunk lid is left open, all of the rest of the sensors attached to the direct input line will be inoperative.

The solution is to give each sensor its own input line by using a multiple differentiator circuit called an *input isolator.* The problem with an input isolator is that it complicates installation by requiring a separate line for each sensor, but the increase in security is worth it.

There are two techniques for isolating multiple inputs on a single line. The first (Fig. 6-13) is an extension of the simple differentiator

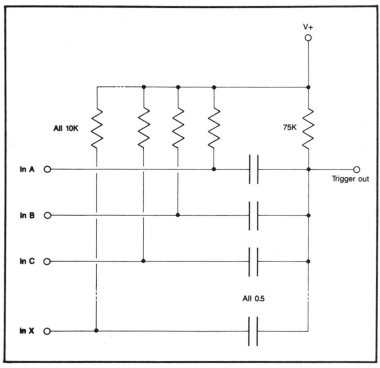

Fig. 6-13. The input isolator allows several input lines to be attached to a single input without their interfering with each other's operation. A latched-low condition on one input will not prevent a low pulse from another input from getting through. Each line is also differentiated, turning a falling edge into a pulse; each line's capacitor and input resistor can also be tailored to its requirements. Up to eight lines may be added to a single input using this circuit.

above. Each sensor has its own pull-up resistor and capacitor, which of course can be tailored to that sensor's characteristics. The other terminals of the capacitors are joined together and use a common pull-up resistor. A negative trigger pulse at any one of the input lines will be passed on to the other side—and to the mainbox—without delay. If one or even more than one of the lines should remain grounded, the others will still be able to transmit their trigger pulses.

The second technique (Fig. 6-14) is a refinement of the first. With the above technique, more than a few capacitors ganged together will start to slow and distort the pulses. If you have, say, eight incoming lines, the total capacitance may be too high for a brief signal to pass through. The solution is to couple each differentiator to a separate input of a CMOS AND gate instead of to each other. The advantage is that each line will still work as before, and still be isolated and unaffected by the states of the other lines, but will not load up the other input lines with excess capacitance. CMOS AND gates are available in 2-, 3-, 4-, and 8-input designs, and they can be tied together to form limitless numbers of other input combinations.

With the AND gate input isolator, the values of the outer resistor and the capacitor can be more or less tailored to the characteristics of the sensor. The inner will have to be duplicated for each line, instead of being common as with the first type of isolator, but can

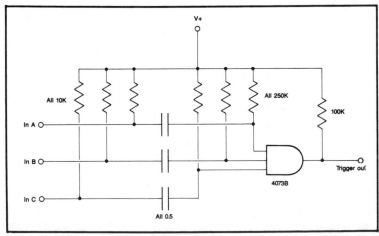

Fig. 6-14. The AND-gate input isolator functions in the same way as the simple input isolator, but is more sensitive and theoretically can be used to add an unlimited number of lines to a single input. A 4073B gate IC is shown, but any CMOS AND gate or combination of AND gates can be used in this circuit. Tie off unneeded gate inputs to V+.

be of a much higher value—from 250K to 1M or even more. Note that a pull-up resistor is used on the AND gate's output: its purpose is to ensure that the trigger input of the mainbox remains high even when the power has just been turned on.

If necessary, the entire input isolator circuit—either type—can be left permanently powered due to its extremely low current draw.

Count Delay

Now, we come to a fundamental problem with all types of automotive security systems. One of the most basic types of sensor is the motion or vibration detector; many off-the-shelf systems use them. The problem is setting their sensitivity levels properly. Too high, and the system's false rate will zoom, too low, and tampering may not trip the alarm.

The elegant solution to this persistent problem is found in the circuit shown in Fig. 6-15, called the count-delay circuit. It is composed of a dual timer and a counter, both CMOS. The count-delay circuit is perhaps the single most important module that can be added to a security system.

When a trigger pulse is received from the motion or vibration sensor, two things happen. First, the two timers are activated, one for a period of 5 to 15 seconds and the other for a period of 0.3 to 0.5 seconds. The long-period timer activates the 4017 counter IC. Second, further trigger impulses will keep retripping the short-period timer, whose output pulses each advance the counter by one count. When the counter reaches its preset count, the output of the circuit will drop low, triggering the mainbox, and in turn the alarm. If the long-period timer times out before sufficient pulses are received, then the circuit will reset.

The way that this circuit increases sensitivity while preventing falses should be obvious. If a passerby or the wind jostles the car, the alarm will not be set off. If, on the other hand, someone is making a determined attempt at theft or vandalism, they will shake the car several times in a row and trip the alarm.

If you have read the book closely up until now, you will immediately appreciate the many facets of this circuit. The most obvious point is that the motion or vibration sensor can be set at a very sensitive level without fear of excessive falses. Debouncing is included by the operation of the short-period timer. To top everything off, not only is the whole circuit superadjustable, but it can be given two or more switch-selectable settings!

The ranges for the short time period, long time period, and

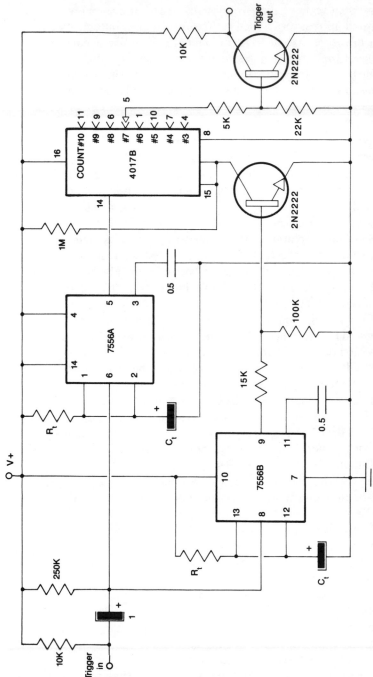

Fig. 6-15. The count-delay circuit. This circuit, used with any motion or vibration sensor, can be adjusted for any time period and number of counts for triggering. Be certain to use the specified 7556 or L556, due to their low current consumption. This circuit should be powered from a switched output of the mainbox so that it shuts down when the system is disarmed. See text for adjustment details.

122

number of counts to triggering are very broad. The recommended settings represent the best compromise for average situations—which of course do not exist. You will have to experiment with various settings to find the best ones for your particular installation.

For the short-period timer the recommended delay period is 0.3 to 1 second. Any shorter than this and one shock to the car may register as two; any longer and two close-together pulses may be registered as one.

For the long-period timer, the recommended delay period is 5 to 20 seconds. Of course, the longer the counting period, the higher the chance that the counter will be advanced to the trigger point. Therefore, for less sensitivity, a shorter period would be used; for more sensitivity, a longer period. Two different periods could be selected by remotely switching between two different timing resistors, or by a voltage applied or not applied to the timer's control input.

The number of counts to triggering can be from two to ten, depending upon which counter output is used to drive the module's trigger output. The recommended number is from three to five, but circumstances can vary. The 0 output cannot be used, since the counter held in reset keeps this output high. Because the first trigger impulse does not advance the counter, the 1 output would go high on the second impulse, the 2 output on the third, and so on up to the 9 output, which would go high on the tenth impulse. It is easy to see how a switch could be used to choose between two outputs to vary the module's sensitivity. The actual means of varying the settings will be covered in Chapter 7.

Between varying the length of the counting period and varying the number of counts required for triggering, almost infinite latitude in sensitivity can be achieved. This circuit eliminates the need for all of the problem-prone newer versions of the motion sensor. This circuit can also make your system many times more flexible.

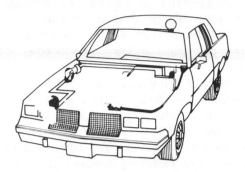

7

Controls and Indicators

T HE CONTROLS AND INDICATORS FOR AN AUTOMOTIVE SECUR-
ity system are at least as important as the modules and sub-
systems that they control and monitor. There are only two basic
types of controls for automotive security systems—the arming/dis-
arming control and the sensitivity-setting selector—but the types,
numbers, and uses of indicators are almost limitless.

In most installations, the controls and indicators will be the only visible parts of the system, and they can be hidden or disguised.
If you don't mind having them out in the open, they shouldn't take
up more than a few square inches of dashboard or console space.
If, on the other hand, you don't want the interior of your classic
car—or your plain old street hauler—disfigured, hiding the controls
and indicators is no problem.

CONTROLS

The most important aspect of controls for automotive security use,
no matter what their function, is their ease of access and usability.
If the arming control or sensitivity selector is too difficult to reach,
or even just a long stretch from the driver's seat, it will quickly
become the tendency not to use the system, or to leave the system
in its lowest sensitivity setting. As with all other parts of the system,
if the controls aren't easy to live with, the system is not properly
designed.

If concealment methods are used, they should accomplish their function without hindering the operation of the controls themselves.

Arming/Disarming Control

The arming/disarming control effectively functions as the security system's on-off switch. In simpler systems, it may actually switch the system's main power on and off; in more complex designs, it will probably switch the system from a low-power-draw standby state to on and vice versa.

There are a number of ways to actually accomplish arming and disarming and they can range from simple to complex in design. They all switch an output between a high and a low level, and the armed or on state can be either level, with the disarmed or off state being its complement. A word of warning, though: arming controls are a common place to get hung up on gimmickry, so take care not to compromise the rest of your system by going overboard in time or money spent on the design of the arming control.

The very simplest type of arming/disarming control is a switch mounted on the outside of the vehicle. This is not a particularly safe way to control your system, since even an inexperienced thief can quickly defeat it. If you have to use an outside switch, do not under any circumstances use a simple toggle or rocker switch. Use only a circular keyswitch with a gasketed weatherproof cover (See Fig. 3-2). The best way to mount an outside keyswitch is inconspicuously, and if possible, blend it into the surface it is mounted in. This can usually be accomplished by painting it body color. (Hint: get a small bottle of touch-up paint from the dealer of your car.) The reason for hiding the switch and indeed concealing the fact that the car is equipped with a security system is that even a pro can be fooled into thinking that the car is unsecured, and will subsequently trip the alarm.

The other side of the coin would be to scare the amateurs and joyriders away by leaving the switch its normal bright chrome and mounting it prominently in the fender or dash well. If you're going to use this technique, reread the last part of Chapter 1 and see if the S.H.A.M. system will fill your needs instead. You might be able to save yourself the cost of a real security system.

Mounting the outside keyswitch is fairly straightforward, as long as you keep two things in mind. First, the switch must be mounted "blind," so that its backside and wiring are concealed and protected by sheet metal or the like. Second, it should be mounted where it is easy to reach and use without going out of your way. Three very good places, in order, are the rear quarter panel (just behind the door), in the cowl panel (just ahead of the windshield), and the front fender. The first is best, since you simply turn one key and then the other, without having to move.

Some other spots that will work, but not as well, are the grille or taillight area (where the switch can be hidden among brightwork), underneath a drip rail, if your vehicle is so equipped, or, in pickups, beneath the rear window, above the bed rail. If the truck is a unibody type, such as a Chevy El Camino, Ford Ranchero, Dodge Rampage, or VW pickup, the switch can be mounted inside the bed itself. Just be sure that it's accessible with the bed loaded and is protected from shifting cargo.

All other types of arming controls are mounted within the passenger area of the vehicle, and subsequently require entry and exit delay timer circuits in the mainbox. The interior type of arming control is vastly superior to the exterior type, since the control itself is protected by the security system.

The best and simplest type of interior arming control is the keyswitch. Mounted on the center console or the dash, the circular type keyswitch will thwart even concerted attacks. With the entry delay ticking away, the alarm will almost certainly sound before the thief can disable the switch.

Mounting the interior keyswitch poses problems similar to those of the exterior type. It must be mounted to resist attempts to tamper with its wiring, and it must be easy to access by the proper person. Most cars have large areas of open space on their dash or console where the switch can be mounted in accordance with these rules.

A subtle trick, one that can be used with the exterior keyswitch as well as with the interior type, is to mount a dummy keyswitch prominently while the real control is hidden. The thief's problems will multiply beyond control if he wastes his time trying to defeat a dummy switch. The cheaper flat-key type switch can be used for dummy purposes.

Another type of arming control, one very commonly found on commercially-built systems, is a fully automatic type requiring no keys or other arming devices. A "deadman" control of the type shown in Fig. 5-11 is wired to the ACCessory terminal of the ignition key. When the ignition is on, or the key is turned to the ACC position, the system will be held disarmed. When the key is turned off, the system's exit delay will count down and arm the system.

This appears, on the surface, to be an excellent way to control the arming of a security system, by using the vehicle's ignition key to do dual duty. It has its pitfalls, though, and these are often overlooked in the glossy advertising that sells so many systems equipped with automatic arming.

First of all, a security system is designed to protect the vehicle it is installed in, regardless of whether the person entering has the proper door and ignition keys. If a thief really wanted a particular car, there are ways that he could duplicate the necessary keys from vehicle ID numbers and the like. (For example, one car company for several years engraved the ignition key's serial number on the inside of the driver's inside door handle. A thief could use an available code book and a keycutter to duplicate the key from the number.)

The second problem with automatic arming is that even an amateur thief can open a door, pull the ignition cylinder, and have the car running within fifteen seconds—well within the range of most entry delay periods.

The automatic arming control falls squarely into the gimmick area, but if you decide that it's for you, keep the entry delay period as short as possible. If you are going to be sitting in the car or unloading packages, you can leave the key turned to the ACC position to keep the system disarmed. It would be a good idea to have a second positive disarming control concealed within the car or under the hood to enable you to disconnect the system altogether at times. For this use, a keyswitch would be a good idea.

A very advanced, tricky arming control, often seen on the more expensive commercial systems such as the Ungo and Clifford, is a combination keypad that requires a code number to be punched in to arm and disarm the system. The great advantage to this type of control is that there are no keys to fumble with or lose. Instead, the numerical code can be made easy to remember and, with most keypad designs, can be changed easily.

There are many designs for electronic combination locks, and most are clumsy, complicated, or difficult to use. The circuit shown in Fig. 7-1 is intended to be easy to build and use, yet high secure. The basic design is for a three-digit code number, but by adding additional 4013B flip-flop ICs, the code can be extended to four, five, six, or seven seven digits. The three-digit code should be enough for most applications, and four or five will be adequate for even high-security applications. The number of keys on the keypad can be any number, as long as there is at least one key for each digit of the code; however, there should be (for highest security) at least two or three keys for each code digit.

This design does not permit the use of any code digit twice in

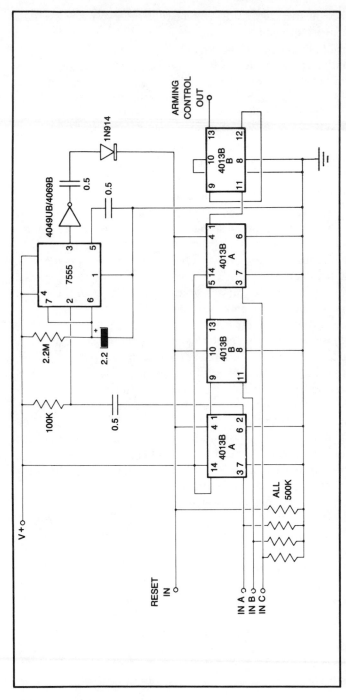

Fig. 7-1. A practical combination keypad circuit. A brief positive pulse at IN A, followed by one at IN B, and then one at IN C, will cause the output flip-flop to change states. The 7555 timer is triggered by the first correct digit and will reset the lock after a five second delay. More flip-flops can be added between the first 'B' flip-flop and the second 'A' flip-flop to increase the number of code digits.

a row. For instance, with a 9-key keypad and a 3-digit code, the combinations 8-6-9, 3-4-3, and 6-3-6 would all be permissible. However, any combination with the same digit twice in a row would not be: 9-9-3, 6-4-4, and 7-4-4 are all invalid codes.

A miniature calculator keyboard is the ideal thing to use for the code keypad. Most surplus electronics stores will have a box or bin full of various designs that can be adapted for automotive security use. Many types can be disassembled, the frame and escutcheon cut to size, and reassembled with the correct number and pattern of keys. The wiring pattern may have to be modified, since most keypads are matrixed, and the needed pattern for this lock is unmatrixed with one side common. This means that each button will in effect be a SPST-NO switch with one lead connected to a common bus and the other lead free of any other connections. Again, the number of keys is up to you, but the more keys and the longer the code, the greater the security. Most calculator keyboards lend themselves well to 9, 12, or 16-key configurations.

If you're interested in calculating the exact number of combinations for any given number of keys and code digits, it's not hard. Since the first digit pressed can be any digit, and all of the rest can be any digit but the last one pressed, it becomes a simple problem in multiplication. Say that you have a 9-digit keypad and a 3-digit code. For the first code digit, you have a choice of any of the nine. For the second, you can choose any but the first digit, or eight, and for the third, again you can choose any but the second, or eight. Therefore, you can have $9 \times 8 \times 8$ or 576 combinations. For a 4-digit code and a 12-button keypad, you would have $12 \times 11 \times 11 \times 11$ possibilities, or over 175,000 combinations!

The operation of the lock is simple: enter the combination once (you have five seconds from the time you hit the first button before the lock resets) and the system will arm; enter it again and the system will disarm. Either the high output or the low output state of the output 4013B can be used as the armed level.

The electronics package should be strongly constructed and mounted in a highly secure location, but should be accessible so that its combination can be changed. The keypad itself can be mounted anywhere that it is convenient. The two modules should be connected with a length of color-coded ribbon cable; one conductor will be required for each key, and one more for the voltage supply.

Figure 7-2 shows the details of construction. The individual leads from the keypad should be plugged into either one of the sequential inputs (if that number is a part of the combination) or into

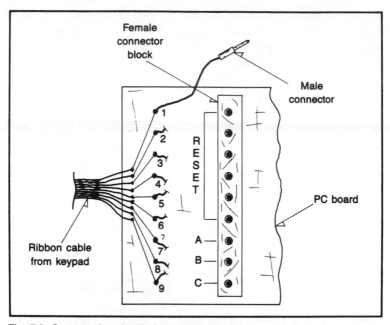

Fig. 7-2. Construction details for the combination keypad. To make the combination changeable, the various leads from the keys should have male connectors on them that can be plugged in at random to a set of female connectors wired to the RESET IN and IN A, B, and C terminals of the circuit of 7-1. Any type of connectors can be used, but a strip of duct tape or other "lock" should be wrapped across the connections so that they cannot accidentally come apart. The entire unit should be built into a strong case and mounted in a location where it would be accessible to change the combination, but safe from tampering.

the reset bus. Only the correct combination and sequence of digits should cause the lock to change states. Any wrong digit immediately resets the lock to its initial state, and any digit of the combination pressed out of sequence will simply have no effect.

Since the keypad electronics are powered continuously, they must be extremely low in current consumption and their power supply very heavily bypassed and filtered. A 2200 μF capacitor, 10 watt zener, and anti-reverse current diodes are the minimum here. A low-current regulation circuit would not be too much to add on top of that.

A very advanced type of arming control is the use of a small radio tone transmitter to switch the system on and off. The most notable use of a control like this is on the Pulsafe security system. With the Pulsafe, you press a button on a tiny hand-held transmitter to arm and disarm the system, even from a distance. When the system is armed, the headlights give a brief flash and the horn beeps to tell the owner that everything is under control. The tricky thing is that the button can be pressed over and over again, even from 100 feet or more away, making the lights and horn flash and beep each time. One of the suggested uses for this feature, in addition to scaring off thieves, is to scare off kids that are using your Porsche 928 as home base for a game of tag.

The concept of a radio arming control is an excellent one, but the transformation from concept to reality is much more difficult. Therefore, no circuitry will be presented here. A discussion of the basics involved is in order for those who wish to design their own, but this project is only recommended for hobbyists with considerable experience in RF electronics.

The FCC rules covering low-power transmitters and the frequencies that they may use are complicated and at times conflicting, but in general, an unlicensed transmitter must have less than 100 milliwatts transmitting power, is restricted to the 27 MHz CB band, and can only use AM modulation. (This roughly defines the hand-held walkie-talkie. Recently, the FCC designated a new frequency for the exclusive use of low-power, unlicensed walkie-talkies.)

For licensed radio-control units, there is a wider choice of frequencies and a higher power limit. There are three frequency bands allotted to radio-control use, such as for model cars and planes: 27, 49, and 72 MHz. These bands are shared with other types of radio devices, so interference is a very real problem; however, FM modulation is allowed.

A simple AM single-tone transmitter is the easiest type of circuit to build, but it leaves too much to be desired for such demanding use. Similarly, a single tone is too low in security, since such a tone could come from an interfering source. The only type of radio arming control device that would be suitable for automotive security use, then, would be suitable for automotive security use, then, would be an FM multiple-tone transmitter. The frequency-modulation delivers a clean, crisp signal under even less-than-ideal conditions, and the multiple tones—whether simultaneous or sequential—act like the digits of a combination to provide high security and prevent anyone from "unlocking" your system—either intentionally or accidentally. The unlicensed limit of 100 milliwatts gives a range of at least 50-100 feet, and should be adequate for most systems. If you require more power, you'll just have to grit your teeth and get the appropriate license. (No test or examination is required, at least.)

Positive indicators of one sort or another should be used, so that you get immediate and absolute feedback telling you that the system is armed or disarmed. The Pulsafe's solution is one way, but audio and visual indicators with less force, such as a buzzer or an LED, can be used.

The great advantage of a radio arming control is that no entry or exit delay is required, and all sensors can be made much more sensitive since you will not need to even touch the car to disarm the system. The disadvantage, perhaps fatal, is that even the best-designed, finest-crafted radio equipment can be temperamental and fail just when you need it. Considering the vagaries of home-brew radio equipment, the simple reliability of a keyswitch begins to look better and better.

One way to avoid being left in the lurch by a malfunctioning radio arming control would be to incorporate a backup disarming control into the system design—such as an exterior keyswitch, or an interior control with the attendant entry and exit delays. Once you have done this, however, the great advantages of the radio control begin to disappear. Perhaps radio arming controls really belong in the gimmick category.

Sensitivity Selector Control

The addition of a sensitivity-varying control to a security system is, bluntly, and excellent idea. It is a much-needed yet rarely-found option on commercially-built systems.

The operation of a sensitivity control is simple. With the turn of a knob or the flip of a switch, the sensitivity of the system's sensor array can be adjusted to a higher or lower setting. The adjustment can be a single step, a series of steps, or even a continuously changing level.

The advantage of a sensitivity control should be obvious: when you park the car or other vehicle in your garage or driveway or other place where it should remain almost completely undisturbed, the control can be set higher. When it is parked in a shopping center or other public place, the control can be adjusted to a lower setting to prevent excessive false alarms.

The mechanics of designing and building a sensitivity control are not difficult. Electronic sensors (or mechanical sensors with electronic processing circuits) can be switched into different levels of sensitivity, and mechanical sensors can be switched in and out of the sensor array.

In practice, sensitivity can be varied in a number of ways. The simplest type of switch would be from, say, a motion sensor set at a high level of sensitivity to another set at a lower level. Another way would be to switch a single motion or vibration sensor in or out of the array altogether.

There are many ways to switch electronic sensors. If your system uses audio or piezo listeners, you could use the sensitivity switch to vary the gain of the amplifier—programmable-gain op-amps are relatively simple devices.

Another way would be to change the settings of the count-delay circuit described in Chapter 6. Instead of setting the long-period counting interval timer and the counter to general purpose settings, you could vary them to give high and low settings. For example, for a low-sensitivity setting, you could set the delay interval at five seconds and/or the number of counts at five. For a higher sensitivity, you could set the counting period at 10 seconds and/or the number of counts at two. In general, it is best to leave the counting interval fairly long—10 seconds or so—and vary the sensitivity by changing the number of trigger counts required.

Given the ease with which a sensitivity control can be added to an automotive security system, there really isn't any reason to compromise with an in-between, all-purpose setting of the system's sensors. The ability to vary the sensitivity of your system will make it many times more flexible—and thus many times more useful.

Concealing and Disguising Controls

Unless you are a technology freak or drive a clunker, you are probably going to want to hide the controls of your security system. There are a number of advantages to concealing your system's controls, and hiding them from a thief is only one. There is only one real disadvantage, and that is that almost any type of concealment will hinder your access. With a little proper design work, though, the concealment shouldn't be too much in the way, and the advantages outweigh the slight access delay.

The biggest advantage is that if the controls aren't in plain sight, then a thief will have that much more trouble finding them—and if he can't find them, he can't tamper with them. A pro will usually be able to figure out concealment methods quickly, and a good amateur won't be far behind, but by concealing the controls you will rob them of precious (entry delay) seconds.

Another advantage to concealing the system's controls is to keep passengers—particularly younger ones—from fiddling with all those interesting little switches and knobs. Ever leave a child in your car, only to later find your stereo's settings totally scrambled?

The third advantage may be the best: appearance. If your car is a particularly fine or sporty model, you will probably not want to foul up the interior with switches and knobs that the stylists never planned on. If your car is a classic or a show car, concealment becomes almost mandatory.

The simplest and most common method of concealing the controls of a security system is to mount them out of sight, for example, under the dash or a seat. The main advantage of this technique is simplicity. However, it violates the principle of making the controls easy to use, since it will be a strain to have to reach up into the guts of your heater every time you want to arm or disarm the system. If you use this concealment method, make sure that first the control is truly hidden and second is not too difficult to reach.

A somewhat difficult but worthwhile concealment method is the "purloined letter" trick. Instead of trying to physically hide the control, make it vanish into the welter of knobs and switches that sprout from your dashboard. If you scour a wrecking yard, you can probably come up with knobs, escutcheon plates, and switch covers that are identical to your existing heater, radio, air conditioner, light, choke, or power window or mirror controls, for example. If you have the available space, no one will question another knob or switch that apparently belongs right where it is. The catch is the last part of that phrase: *apparently belongs right where it is.* A light switch above the radio or a radio knob on the transmission hump are not apparently anything but stupid. Used properly, the purloined letter method is an excellent one; used wrong and you may as well stick with exposed controls.

The final concealment method is to simply cover the controls with a panel or cover. It is not suited to cars with fine interiors that would be marred by any additions—such as a Jaguar with a carved walnut dashboard. For all other types of cars, it should work well. After all, it's the most obvious solution: just put the controls where they work and then cover them!

It is no great problem to make or find a small recessed area to mount a keyswitch or keypad and such. Many late-model cars purchased with less than every available option have snap-in covers or empty depressions in the dash where the option or its control would have gone—a disgusting practice at best, but one that can be turned to the advantage of the security system designer. If your vehicle is free of extraneous depressions on its interior, a small plastic or aluminum project box can be used instead. It simply must be mounted securely in a closely-fitted hole at the appropriate spot in the dash or console.

Whether in place or added, the necessary holes for mounting the controls are drilled or cut and the controls are mounted in place. If the box or depression is too deep, a mounting plate can be cut to fit and fastened in place using small bolts and spacers.

The cover for the controls is the most critical part of an installation of this type. In most cases, it should not be concealed. For example, if the box or depression is in the center of the vinyl dash pad, don't use a matching piece of vinyl stock to make the cover—such a cover would be spotted instantly by both child and thief alike.

Instead, use a contrasting material of a type that looks plausible in your dash or wherever. If your car, for example, has wood-grain trim along with the vinyl dash, use a neatly-edged piece of matching wood-grain as the cover. In a sports or muscle car, a piece of brushed or anodized aluminum will look right at home. In classic cars, you can use a piece of 1/8-inch veneer plywood to make the cover.

Use your imagination and dig through the wrecking yards to come up with bits and pieces of trim materials that you can use for covers. Just keep it all plausible.

In most cases, a simple cover like the above will be sufficient. In some cars, though, a simple cover of any type may be too conspicuous. In those cases, turn the cover into a plaque—use the plastic, metal, or wood surface to mount something else. A copy of the car's logo or the manufacturer's emblem, mounted neatly in the center of the cover, will effectively conceal the surface's true nature. (Is it necessary to add that suitable badges, logos, and emblems can be found at the local wrecking yard?) As an alternative, find a piece elsewhere on your vehicle that will work and then order a copy from the dealer.

Instead of a logo, of course, you can use just about anything: a decal of your astrological sign, Ziggy, Garfield, a "happy face," or whatever strikes your personal fancy. Small press-on and stick-on letters can be used as well to make up more individual messages.

The cover itself should be mounted to the dash or console surface using small spring-loaded hinges or simple hinges and a magnetic catch. The spring-loaded type with a magnetic catch would be even better. Both should be available at any hobby shop or cabinet maker's supply store.

INDICATORS

Almost all automotive security systems beyond the most basic types will demand the use of one or more indicators. An indicator can be nearly any type of visual or audible signal, and can be used to tell you nearly anything about the state of your system.

There are a number of basic designs for lamp, LED, and audible-tone indicators, and each can be hooked into your system with a little forethought and ingenuity. As with sensors, where you can find or design one to detect nearly anything, an indicator can be found or designed to tell you nearly anything!

Visual Indicators

The light-emitting diode, or LED was made for automotive use. It is small, extremely durable, and has a virtually indefinite life. Fig. 7-3 illustrates some of the different types available. They can be commonly found in four colors: red, green, yellow, and amber. There are a number of gradations and variations among the last two colors such as yellow, orange, amber, yellow-orange, amber-orange, and almost any other combination. LEDs are also available in a wide range of sizes, from the large TI-1 3/4 "tophat" to tiny specks with hair-fine leads. In general, the larger sizes will be needed in an automotive application because of their greater visibility.

The LED is a small diode junction encased in a plastic substrate. All LEDs emit a tiny point of light, with the brightness of the point being determined by the size of the junction and the current level

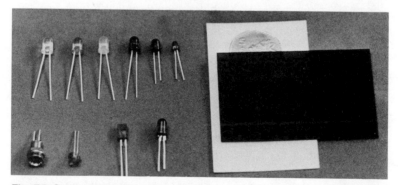

Fig. 7-3. Some of the various types of LEDs available are shown here. Starting at the top left, the first four are jumbo TI-1 3/4 types in clear, green, amber, and red lenses; the next two are miniature and subminiature red types; on the bottom row, a green LED in a chrome bezel; a fresnel-lensed green; a rectangular red, and an FRL flashing red type with integral CMOS flasher IC. The dark oblong at right is a red LED contrast filter. The 5-peso piece is not an indicator.

being passed through it. LEDs can be had in clear cases that do not expand the tiny point, or in diffused cases (or lenses, to be more correct) that spread the point of light out into a larger light. The plastic of the lens can be either clear or colored. In the clear lenses, the LED will appear its natural color, and in the colored lenses, it will appear to be the same color as the lens. The LED's color will usually be the same as the color of the lens, though. For automotive use, the best combination is a clear diffused-lens unit with a large lens area. The color can be chosen to suit your needs and fancies.

In addition to the standard range of LEDs, there are a number of unusual designs that may find application in your system. The first is a fresnel-lens design that uses the fresnel-type lens to give the light of the LED an even bigger area than the tophat style. It has a flat face a quarter of an inch across, and is highly recommended for automotive use. Another type is the rectangular LED, which can be stacked end-to-end or side-by-side to create either a bargraph type display or even to give you a single enormous LED.

A very interesting type of LED is the Litronix FRL flashing type. This unit combines an LED junction and a tiny CMOS IC in a standard tophat lens. When 5 volts is applied to the unit's terminals, the LED will flash at a 2-3 Hz rate, without the use of external components. There is only one restriction regarding the use of the flashing LED: it must have a 5-volt power source. A simple dropping resistor will not do, and the application of more than 5 volts will burn out the internal IC. A simple resistor-zener network, or one of the regulated outputs shown in Chapter 5 is adequate, and no current-limiting is required.

LEDs do have some drawbacks. They need a fair amount of current, from 10 to 50 milliamps, and so cannot be used for continuous duty. Most LEDs used in automotive security systems will not need to remain lit for more than a few seconds, however, so this problem need not be limiting.

All LEDs, with the exception of the flashing type, must have current limiting. An LED operates on 1.5 to 2 volts. Since the voltage that powers them is often considerably higher, a series resistor must be used. To calculate the value of the resistor, you need to know two things: the LED's voltage drop and how much current you want it to use. Most LEDs need at least 10 milliamps to be visible, and most can handle up to 50 milliamps for the best visibility. Thirty milliamps is a good, all-around figure.

The LED's voltage drop can be measured by hooking a representative type (of the same color and size) up to a 9-12 volt source with a 1K series resistor. Measure the voltage across the LED's terminals; this is its voltage drop. Most red LEDs have a drop of 1.5 volts; most green ones, 2 volts; most yellow ones, 1.7 volts.

Once you have the two figures, you can calculate the series resistor's value using the formula:

$$R_{LED} = \frac{(V+) - (V_{LED})}{I_{LED}}$$

V+ is the nominal system voltage, V_{LED} is the LED's voltage drop, R_{LED} is the series resistor's value (in ohms), and I_{LED} is the selected LED current in amperes (i.e., 30 milliamps would be used here as 0.030 amps). The R_{LED} designation will be found on almost every schematic in this book that uses an LED. Refer to this formula when needed.

A far more serious drawback to LEDs is their poor visibility in high ambient light conditions. If the interior of the car is brightly lit by the sun or even by a powerful streetlight, the LED may be washed out and its condition—on or off—impossible to determine. The problem can be solved by two tricks. First, all LEDs used should be mounted in a deep well or depression where they are in the driver's line of sight. The well should be in shadow most of the time. Second, a contrast filter should be used over all LEDs. A contrast filter is simply a piece of colored plastic that heightens the contrast between the lit and non-lit areas of the indicator area. A deep mounting and a contrast filter will serve to eliminate washout under most circumstances.

There is a third trick to prevent washout. The flashing LED can often be seen even in bright sunlight. The eye could not determine if it was simply on or off, but the continuous alternation would be readily evident. A flashing LED behind a contrast filter would be even better. The fresnel-lensed LEDs also have excellent highlight visibility. The ultimate LED indicator, then, would be a fresnel-lensed LED behind a contrast filter, with circuitry to make it flash.

Mounting LEDs is simple. There are a number of off-the-shelf mounts for nearly all lens styles of LEDs, from simple plastic clips to threaded metal bezels. Alternately, you can simply glue the LED into its mounting surface using either a plastic cement or a cyanoacrylate superglue.

Incandescent bulbs, although they draw a tremendous amount of current—often 250 to 500 milliamps—have one great advantage over LEDs: visibility. An incandescent in a lensed mount can be seen clearly even under the highest ambient light conditions. Many styles and colors of mounts are available.

Audio Indicators

Aural or audio indicators are an alternative to visible types. They can be used instead of or even with a visible type, if necessary. The great advantage to the audible type is that it can be made completely hidden—a necessity in some cars.

There are three types of audible indicators. The simplest to use and the cheapest is the mechanical buzzer (Fig. 7-4). This type can be found in a huge variety of sizes, voltages, and tones. Their drawbacks are that they draw a fair amount of current and generate a lot of hash and noise on the power line. If a mechanical buzzer is used, make sure to use a bypass diode across its terminals—since it is basically a coil device that generates semiconductor-destroying spikes—and a capacitor or other bypassing device to keep the hash from filtering back to the security system's circuitry.

The second type of audible indicator is the piezoelectric tone generator (Fig. 7-5). They are somewhat more expensive than the mechanical types, but they draw less power and have a more ear-pleasing sound, unlike the harsh rasp of the mechanical buzzers.

There are two types of piezo buzzers, those that are internally driven—where you just supply power and they make noise—and the somewhat more flexible externally-driven type. The latter needs at least a simple circuit to drive it, but the advantage is that you can

Fig. 7-4. Some of the types of mechanical buzzers available. They are inexpensive, but have several problems that limit their use—see text.

Fig. 7-5. Piezoelectric buzzers use less power and have a more pleasing sound than mechanical types. The piezo element on the left requires a driver circuit, unlike the all-in-one type. The Mallory Sonalert on the right is an example of the latter.

vary its tone and have more control over turning it on and off.

The third type of audible indicator is an oscillator/speaker device. The disadvantage of this type is its complexity—often two dozen or more components—but its advantage is flexibility. Using

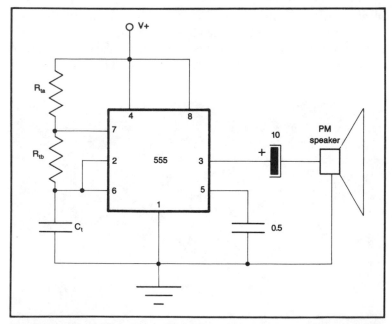

Fig. 7-6. Oscillator/driver for audio indicator use. A 555 by itself can produce any single tone desired by varying the two timing resistors and the timing capacitor, as well as directly drive a small permanent-magnet speaker. For higher volume, the 10 μF capacitor can be increased up to 35 μF.

a tiny speaker, from 1 to 2 inches in size, you can generate nearly any sounds or combinations of sounds that you can imagine. A single speaker and drive circuit could be made programmable so that several indicator inputs would produce many different tones or sounds.

For a driver circuit, a single 555 or a dual 556 timer IC can be used. The 555, like that in Fig. 7-6, can produce any single tone desired, and the 556, Fig. 7-7, can produce a wide range of sounds from simple two-tone to the more bizarre.

If you really want to get involved and inventive, you could give your security system a voice. The recent advent of single-chip voice synthesizers makes it possible to add a module that would literally tell you "security system is arming" or "security system is activated" or "security system has been disarmed." The possibilities are endless. Unfortunately, so are the complexities. Avoid getting hung up on the voice synthesizer to the point of gimmickry. (Incidentally, the now-feasible concept of a voice-synthesis circuit in an automotive security system raises some interesting ideas about the alarm output. How about a system that screams "This car is being stolen!" at 120 decibels? See Chapter 8 for a further discussion.)

Using Indicators

As mentioned at the head of this chapter, indicators can be developed to indicate practically anything. The most common uses for indicators are outlined here, but don't let this short list limit your own imagination and needs.

The basic idea is to pick a particular signal—almost always a simple high or low one—and use it to turn whatever type of indicator you choose on or off. In most if not all cases, it will be necessary to use a CMOS 4049 or 4050 buffer to keep the indicator circuit from loading and distorting the original signal. Note that this is not shown on the indicator schematics.

There are three basic types of indicator driver circuits: simple, driven, and latching. The simple type (Fig. 7-8) is connected directly to the driving source. It is not useful in most situations. The driven type (Fig. 7-9) is the most common type. A transistor, which may or may not be driven by a CMOS buffer, is the actual current source for the indicator. The latching type (Fig. 7-10) is similar to the driven type in that current is sourced indirectly, but once it receives an on signal, it will latch the indicator on until the voltage to the indicator circuit is broken.

Note that for illustration purposes in Figs. 7-8, 7-9, and 7-10

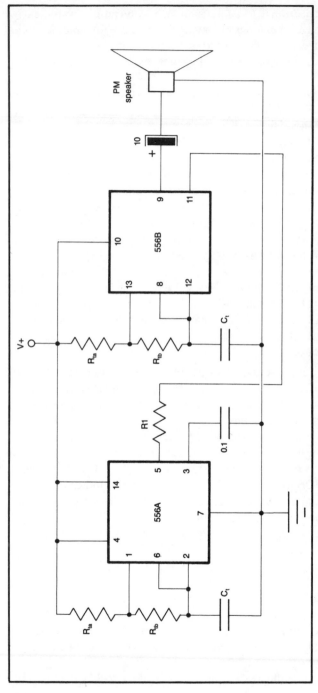

Fig. 7-7. This 556-based oscillator can produce an unbelievable range of sounds, from two-tone to way-out. The second oscillator's output is modulated by the first oscillator's output. The tones and sounds can be modified by varying the timing elements and R1, the latter from 0-100K. This is a good circuit to experiment with on a solderless breadboard, using pots for R1 and both R_{ib}'s to develop a one-of-a-kind sound. The circuit should then be constructed with fixed resistors. (Note that these circuits are also used in Chapter 8, without the output capacitor and speaker, as drive elements for alarm output use. Experimentation would be called for there, too.)

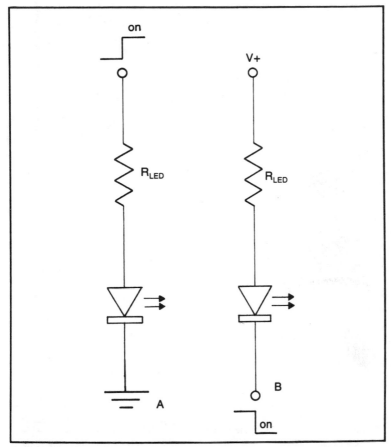

Fig. 7-8. Simple indicators are driven directly from the source, and have limited use.

the indicator shown is an LED (and its attendant resistor). These can be replaced by an incandescent lamp or a buzzer without modification of the circuit. The only thing to keep in mind is that the output transistor or SCR must be able to handle the current of the indicator.

Probably the most fundamental use of an indicator is as an arming indicator. This type will tell you when the system is arming, armed, and even disarmed—although a disarmed indicator is usually a separate unit.

The usual way to implement an arming indicator is to pick off the exit delay timer's output signal. In most systems, the signal will be high while the system is counting down towards arming, and low

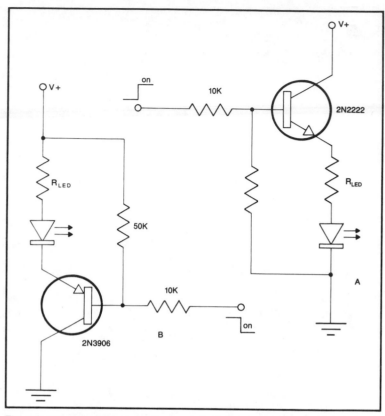

Fig. 7-9. Driven indicators are the most flexible type of indicator. Be sure that the transistor used has sufficient current capability to drive the indicator, and be sure to use a bypass diode if the indicator involves a coil of any type. A CMOS buffer is recommended on the input to keep from loading the circuit that provides the signal.

afterwards. Therefore, it would be used directly—with appropriate buffering and amplification—to drive the indicator.

In operation, the act of turning the arming control to the armed position would cause the indicator to light or begin sounding off. When the system is actually armed, the light or noise would stop.

While either an LED or a buzzer is all right for arming indicator use, the best of all would be a flashing, red LED. If the system were to become accidentally armed while driving, the flashing light would attract immediate attention. If you so wished, you could mount the indicator where it could be seen from the outside of the car. Then, you could turn the key or punch in your code, get immediate visual feedback that arming was indeed underway, get out, and get im-

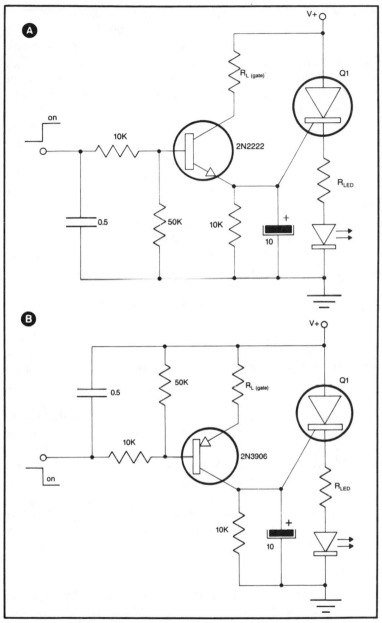

Fig. 7-10. A latching indicator will stay on even after the trigger signal returns to normal. A sensitive-gate SCR should be used; $R_{1\ (gate)}$ is used to limit its gate current to an acceptable figure. Be certain that these circuit's V+ is interrupted by disarming, so that they can unlatch. CMOS buffering of the inputs is recommended.

mediate visual feedback when arming was complete.

An excellent addition to any system equipped with an exit/entry delay is a disarm-reminder indicator. This type of indicator would light or sound off when the output of the entry delay goes high, which is obviously after the system has been triggered through the delayed trigger input. Again, the signal should be buffered to prevent malfunctions.

In operation, the indicator would light or begin to sound off when the system has begun its countdown towards the alarm state, reminding you as you get in to disarm the system. Either a visual or audio type can be used, but an audio is recommended. If your vehicle has seatbelt or ignition-key buzzers, make sure to make the disarm-reminder's tone distinctive and loud enough to be heard over them.

Obviously, no system needs an indicator to tell the operator that the system is in the alarm state—the noisemakers and flashing lights will do quite well! However, it would be nice to have an indicator that would tell you if the system has gone into the alarm state in your absence. Even if your system is equipped with a pager, an alert indicator is a good idea, since it is no trick to get out of range of the pager's transmitting area.

The alert indicator is easy enough to add to any system. Simply use the buffered latching type indicator circuit of Fig. 7-10 to drive an LED—yellow is the color of choice—and pick the drive signal from the alarm output. When the system goes into the alarm state, it will latch the indicator on.

One word of warning: keep the indicator's current draw to an absolute minimum. Since it may remain on for as long as a day or more, excessive current could cause a dead battery. Ten milliamps is the maximum; to make sure that the LED is visible with such a low drive current, use a carefully selected mounting location and a contrast filter.

If you should ever find the indicator lit, take it as a warning and use extra caution in parking and watching your car for a few days or weeks. A pro could be casing you and may return prepared to defeat the system. A lit alert indicator could also mean that an auto burglar has cleaned the car out—in which case you can take a quick inventory and report any loss that much faster.

A sensor status indicator is a useful addition to any system. It will tell the operator during the exit delay period whether or not all of the sensors are in the off state. It's not a simple indicator to add, but it's worth it.

Since most systems have several trigger input lines, some sort of multiplexer will have to be added to the indicator's input. Each trigger line has to be isolated from the others and still be monitored for a low closed sensor state, so the best multiplexing device would be a CMOS NAND gate (see Fig. 7-11). As long as all of the gate's inputs are high, its output will be low. If any of the inputs should drop low, its output will go high. The CMOS inputs will not load the trigger inputs, of course. If the system has only a single trigger input, a simple CMOS buffer can be used instead.

The input or inputs of the buffer or gate should be connected directly to the incoming trigger lines, before any input conditioning or other circuitry. The output of the gate or buffer should be used to drive a driven indicator circuit like that in Fig. 7-9A. Either an LED or a buzzer can be used as the output device.

The circuit should draw its power from the mainbox's V+ bus so that it goes on and off with the system. Normally, the indicator will be enabled whenever the system is armed. In systems using an entry/exit delay, no further components are necessary. In systems lacking an entry/exit delay, the circuit should be powered directly from V+ and a pushbutton added to give on-demand status readings.

The operation of the sensor status indicator is straightforward. When the button is pushed or the system is armed, assuming all of the doors are closed, the sensor should remain off. In systems that do not require a button, arm the system as usual and get out. As the doors are opened and the motion sensor jiggled, the indicator

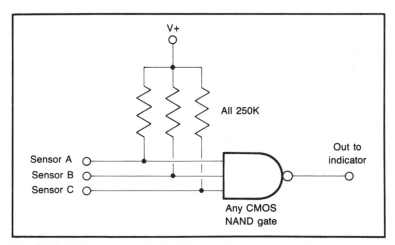

Fig. 7-11.A sensor status indicator will let you know immediately if any sensors are in the triggered state. Any B-series CMOS NAND gate can be used to give the needed number of inputs; it should be used to drive indicator 7-9A for best results.

will light. When you and your passengers are all out and the doors are shut, the indicator should go out within a few seconds. If it does not, there is a sensor in the closed position somewhere and the system will go immediately into the alarm state upon arming. If this happens, quickly check the vehicle for an open door, trunk, hood, or other similar condition that would cause a sensor to be in the open position. If no obvious condition is found, disarm the system and check things out a little more thoroughly.

A disarmed indicator is a nice addition, giving a positive feedback when the system is disarmed. When the system is properly disarmed, it will go on for a few seconds to tell you that the system has indeed shut down. It is almost a mandatory addition, along with an arming indicator, for automatic-arming systems.

The simplest design for a disarmed indicator (Fig. 7-12) is a low-power 555 timer (a 7555 or L555), permanently powered, with its trigger connected to the mainbox's internal power supply bus. When the system is disarmed and the power to the mainbox cuts off, the timer will be triggered and its output will go high for its selected time period. A green LED is the best choice, although any other color—or a buzzer—can be used. As with the combination keypad, since this unit is powered all of the time, use very heavy filtering

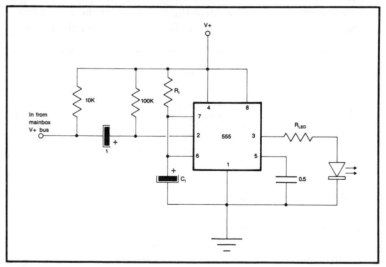

Fig. 7-12. A disarmed indicator goes on briefly to let you positively know that the system has been disarmed. A 7555 or L555 must be used, since the circuit is permanently powered. The MAINBOX V+ IN terminal should be connected to a point within the mainbox that is switched on and off by arming and disarming.

148

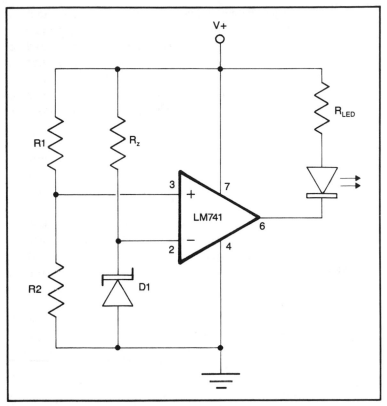

Fig. 7-13. The voltage-warning indicator will go on to tell you that your backup battery has dropped to an abnormally low level. It simplifies checking up on things when the car is not driven frequently, but its adjustment is tricky.

and bypassing to prevent false triggering. The low-power timer IC is required, since the circuit is continuously powered.

If your system uses a backup power supply, an indicator that tells you its status is a good idea. The simple op amp circuit in Fig. 7-13 will light an LED if the backup battery's voltage falls below a preset level, and so warn you that there is a problem with current draw or the backup charging circuitry. The zener D1's voltage can be any value around 30-50 percent of the normal supply voltage; R_z should limit current to a minimum—around 100K or so is about right. R1 and R2 should total about 250K, and a 250K pot can be used for adjustment.

Set the pot in the middle of its travel and power up the circuit using the exact voltage at which you want the indicator to light up (85 percent of the nominal V+ is a good figure). Adjust the pot so that the indicator just comes on; raise the supply voltage to the normal supply level. The indicator should be dark. Slowly reduce the voltage to the circuit until the LED lights; the supply voltage should be very close to the warning level selected. Replace the pot with 1-watt metal-film resistors for stability.

There are two ways to use this indicator: automatic or on-demand. With the first method, the circuit is simply wired across the system's power supply bus, and if the battery's voltage ever drops too far, it will light. The second method is to wire it through a pushbutton, so that a reading is only taken when the button is pushed.

The disadvantage of the automatic type is that it draws a small amount of current continuously, which may be unacceptable; the disadvantage of the on-demand type is that you have to remember to push the button regularly to check the battery. Remember, the indicator will not give a correct reading when the engine is running unless there is a problem between the main electrical system and the backup.

If your vehicle is equipped with a voltmeter (as opposed to an ammeter, a truly useless gauge), you can wire it with a SPDT pushbutton so that it will read out the backup's voltage on demand. The problem here is the same as the pushbutton version of the indicator above: you have to remember to push the button frequently.

Mounting Indicators

Mounting indicators should not present much of a problem. Most of the principles already discussed in connection with mounting controls will apply to indicators as well. The mounts that can be used with visual indicators have also already been discussed. Most audible indicators have mounting provisions as part of their case, and those that you construct yourself can be built with screw ears on theirs.

The big question is where to mount the indicators. Audible types can be mounted almost anywhere that they are out of sight, such as up inside the dashboard. It would be almost impossible to mount an audible indicator so that it would not be heard, but keep it in front of air conditioning ducts and heavy wiring bundles, just to be safe.

Mounting visual indicators is trickier. If you have your controls out in the open, the indicators can be neatly mounted alongside them using standard panel-mounting hardware. If such a mounting job is clean enough, they will appear to be part of the original equipment of the car. If your controls are hidden, however, you will have to make a choice.

One method would be to place the indicators in the same hiding place as the controls. Since some of the indicators need to be visible more or less at all times, a tinted lens would have to be part of the cover of the hiding place. The lens could be made into part of the design disguising the cover.

Another method would be to use subminiature LEDs and mount them in tiny holes on the edge of the dash pad or even within the faces of the vehicle's instruments, or—even better—on the face of the vehicle's clock. When unlit, they will be almost invisible, and when lit, they should be clearly visible—if you know where to look. To a thief or other unauthorized person, they will appear to be part of the car's regular equipment.

8

Warning Devices

THE FINAL STAGE OF AN AUTOMOTIVE SECURITY SYSTEM IS its output warning devices. They can be noise, lights, radio signals, or even a little black box that disables the car. Regardless of the type, a security system's output devices are ultimately the protecting parts of the system.

Obviously, the purpose of noise and flashing lights is to attract attention from police, security guards, and passersby, and to frighten away thieves and vandals. The purpose of a radio-paging device is to let you know that there's a problem—even if you are miles away. And the purpose of a disabling device is to ensure that even a determined thief won't be able to just drive the car away, despite the noise and lights.

Because the output and warning devices are the actual protection-giving portion of the system, they deserve both a little care in their design and a little extra cash in the purchase of their parts. Warning devices are often the single most expensive portion of an automotive security system.

POWER-SWITCHING CIRCUITRY

In Chapter 5, it was mentioned that the alarm output of the main-box should be limited to 200 or 300 milliamperes. Obviously, there must be some intermediate step between this relatively low-power signal and the high-power output devices. The intermediate step is a *power switch*. There are several different designs for power switches, and all have their own advantages and disadvantages.

Transistor Design

The transistor-based design for power switches is for low to moderate current sourcing with a minimum of standby and operating current draw. Although very-high-power transistors are available, the design should be limited to carrying levels of two amps or less and the driving transistor should be highly derated and use a large heatsink. A large finned or vaned aluminum heatsink should be used, not a clip-on type.

There are two basic designs for a transistor power switch, the one-transistor and two-transistor types. The single-transistor design (Fig. 8-1) is adequate for low-current switching, up to 500 milliamps, but the two-transistor type (Fig. 8-2) is recommended for all applications.

Both designs use a power transistor to do the actual heavy-duty switching work. The difference is that the single-transistor type uses the alarm output signal directly to drive the power transistor, while

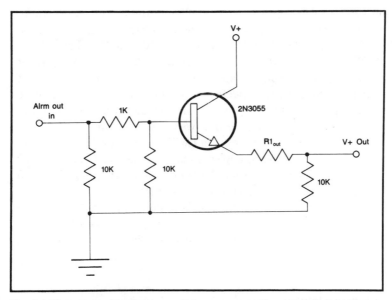

Fig. 8-1. The one-transistor power switch can be used for switching light loads— up to 500 mA—but is not really a recommended design. The 2N3055 must be heatsunk. Note that no bypassing diode is shown; one must be added if the circuit drives an inductive load. The two-transistor power switch (Fig. 8-2) is the preferred design.

153

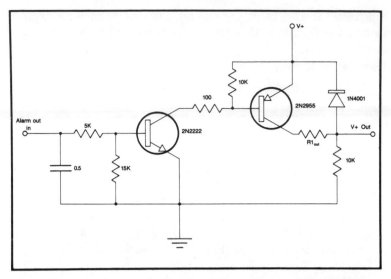

Fig. 8-2. The two-transistor type power switch in an adequate design for switching up to 2 amperes. The output 2N2955 transistor requires a heatsink. The diode can be omitted if the circuit is not driving an inductive load.

the two-transistor unit uses a smaller buffer/driver transistor to isolate the power transistor from the drive signal. The latter type operates more cleanly, with a more positive on/off switch.

The critical factor for the design of both types is the current load rating of the power transistor. The I_c of the transistor must be at least double the expected maximum load. This is one case where very large derating factors are not out of place: 200-1,000 percent is the kind of range that we're talking about.

The transistor's voltage rating will not usually be a problem, although some very large power transistors may have ratings of 12 volts or less. Make sure that the transistor's rating is at least 25 volts for all applications, and higher is better.

Another critical factor for transistor power switch design is the bypassing of the power transistor. Even heavy-duty power transistors are prone to transient damage, and so a spike-bypassing diode across the transistor's emitter and collector is required.

Thyristor Design

Thyristors make a better power switch than transistors in some cases. Since triacs and SCRs are latching semiconductors, they must power devices that break their own circuits, such as mechanical

154

(motorized) sirens, bells, and circuits that incorporate a thermal flasher. When used in such a way, the circuit or device will remain powered as long as the gate of the thyristor has the proper voltage level, and will be cut off when the gate's level switches to the opposite state. The advantage of a thyristor over a transistor is that very-high-power SCRs and triacs are quite readily available, while high-power transistors are hard to find and expensive.

The actual design of thyristor power switches is very similar to that of the transistor types. When a triac is used, either of its two orientations can be used—high-trigger or low-trigger—whichever makes the most sense for your design. Both the SCR power switch (Fig. 8-3) and the triac type (Fig. 8-4) should use a small buffer transistor on their input.

SCRs should have a spike-bypassing diode across its terminals; triacs are inherently immune to transient damage and no such bypassing is needed for them.

Relay Design

Although relays are primarily designed for switching, a relay type power switch is a more difficult piece of equipment to design

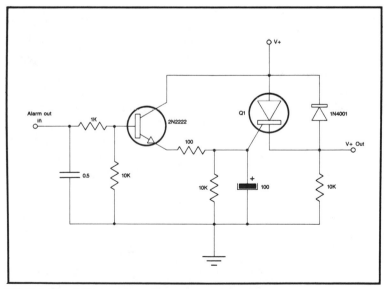

Fig. 8-3. The SCR-based power switch can be used to drive any device that breaks its own circuit—bells, motorized sirens, flashers—with lower dissipation than a transistor type. The device to be powered should be test-driven with an SCR to make sure that it does indeed unlatch.

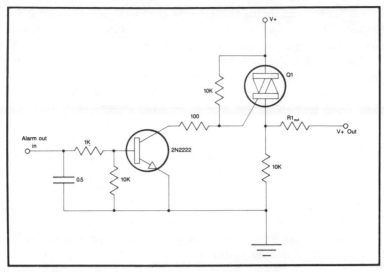

Fig. 8-4. The triac-based power switch operates similarly to the SCR type, but the triac can be used in a high-trigger mode (identical to Fig. 8-3 without the bypassing diode) or the simpler low-trigger mode shown here.

and build than are the above solid-state types. The reason is that the solid-state types are built from scratch and can be modified and redesigned easily. Relays, on the other hand, are not generally available to the hobbyist in more than a few types and contact configurations, and so compromises must be made in the design of a relay power switch.

Despite the problems, relay-type power switches have a few great advantages. First, relays can handle very large amounts of current with very little dissipation. Also, since the contacts of a relay are nothing more than an ordinary switch, their switching is non-polarized. Therefore, for power-switching applications that call for direct nonpolarized or high-current switching, a relay-based power switch is called for.

The problem with relays, as mentioned earlier in the book, is the difficulty of finding units with both low-current coils and high-current contacts. The compromise cannot be made in the contacts—you simply can't switch 5 amps with a 1-amp set of contacts—so it must be in the coil. For power switch use, choose a relay whose contacts fit the need first and then worry about the coil current. Just make an effort to keep the latter as low as possible. For a very high contact current capability, from 10 to 20 amps, you may have to put up with a 500 milliamp coil current.

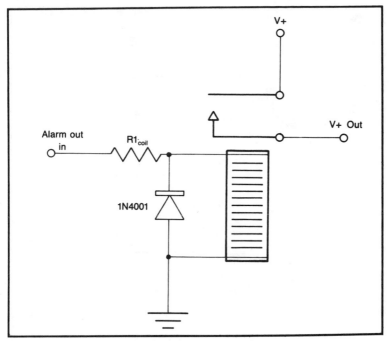

Fig. 8-5. A simple relay power switch can be made with only three components.

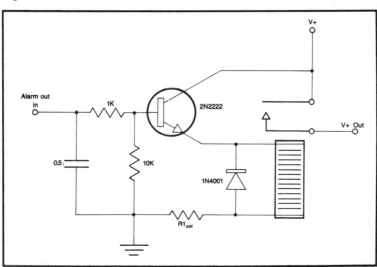

Fig. 8-6. A buffered relay mainbox has all of the advantages of using a relay as a switching element, but lowers the current drawn from the mainbox's output. Note that no output limiting resistor is shown on either this circuit or the one in Fig. 8-5; one should be used if the device powered draws more than 50 percent of the contacts' rated current.

157

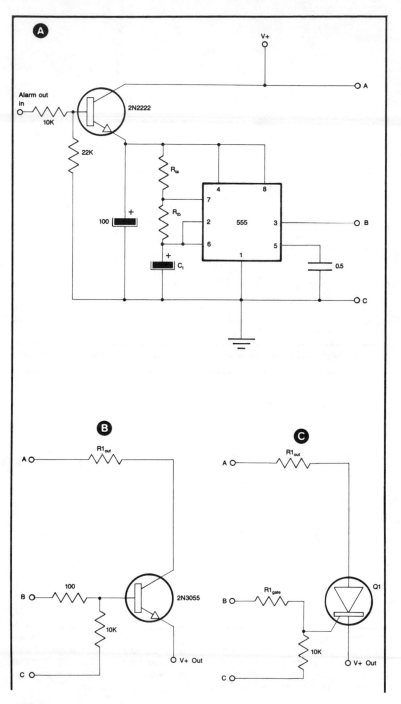

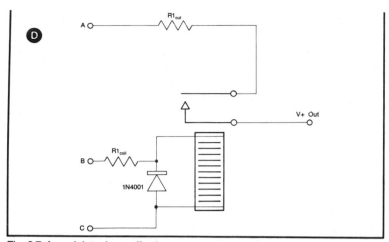

Fig. 8-7. A modulator is an effective way to make any alarm output more attention-getting. The basic circuit in Fig. 8-7A is a buffered 555 astable. It should be set for a 0.2 to 5 Hz rate, depending on the type of output device driven. It can use any of three outputs: (B) a transistor for up to two-amp devices (C) an SCR for self-breaking devices up to 10 amps (D) a relay for nonpolarized switching up to 20 amps.

A simple power switch (Fig. 8-5) can be made from a relay and two other components, but to minimize current load on the main-box's output, a driver circuit must always be used on the relay's input (Fig. 8-6). A simple single-transistor type is sufficient, but remember that it must have bypass diode across its terminals to protect it from the spikes generated by the relay coil.

Modulators

A modulator is a special type of power switch that does not just turn the alarm device on and then off as the alarm output signal dictates, but pulses it on and off in a fast 1—2 Hz rhythm for the alarm period. The reason for doing this is to make a steady sound or a commonplace sound more distinctive and attention-getting. It can also be used to flash lights in lieu of a thermal-type flasher.

The design of a modulator is simple, as Fig. 8-7A shows. The heart of it all is a 555 timer wired as an astable with a period of 0.1 to 5 Hz, with the actual setting to be determined by the use. For some uses, an asymmetrical output may even be desired. The timer is turned on and off by the alarm output signal, and its output in turn is used to drive any type of high-current drive element—a transistor (Fig. 8-7B), thyristor (Fig. 8-7C), or relay (Fig. 8-7D). The timer section of the modulator should have fairly heavy bypassing to keep the spikes and hash from the driven alarm device from messing up its rhythm.

It should be kept in mind that besides the addition of an astable timer, a modulator is still a power switch and all applicable design rules and restrictions for each type of output still apply. In addition, the current ratings of the output device should be increased above the already high level, since the repeated surge currents may be a higher average figure than a steady current.

ALARMS

The most fundamental of all types of warning devices are alarms. Alarms are any type of electronic or mechanical equipment that warn you, or the police, or passersby. They include sirens, bells, horns, flashing lights, radio-pagers, etc.

Noisemakers

Noisemakers are the most fundamental of warning devices. A horn, siren, or bell is often the central—or only—warning device on nearly all automotive security systems. There are dozens of different specific types, each with its own strengths and weaknesses. Some are cheap, some not so cheap, and some can double the cost of your system in one whack. In general though, extra money put into a noisemaking device is money well spent.

The most critical factor to consider in selecting a noisemaking device for your system is its loudness in decibels. An in-depth discussion of decibels is found in Chapter 3. Essentially, the rule is the louder the better, with few exceptions.

Horns are the simplest type of noisemaking device. There are two types: the vehicle's existing mechanical horn and airhorns. The end result is much the same with both types, with the difference being that airhorns are louder and have a clearer tone. A big horn of either type can be a real earsplitter, which is just what you're trying to achieve. A big mechanical truck horn can hit 110 decibels, and big airhorn can pump out 120 or more!

The problem with horns of either type and even high power is that their sound is too commonplace and may not be recognized as an alarm signal. The beeps and blats of horns are a common sound in most cities, and even a long steady blare from an airhorn may just produce irritation in those within earshot. One way to improve the alarm characteristics of a horn is to use a modulator to pulse it on and off. Such a loud, pulsing noise would attract more attention than a steady, unwavering one.

Most mechanical horns are of the buzzer type. They have a set of points that open and close rapidly, like a mechanical buzzer. If a single horn of this type is used, a thyristor power switch may also be used. Most airhorns have a small motor-driven compressor to source them their air, and it may be possible to use a thyristor power switch with them. For very-high-power horns, it may be necessary to use a relay-type power switch. In general, airhorns use less power to generate more decibels than the mechanical types.

Bells are a much-overlooked noisemaking device for automotive security systems. They are fairly cheap, loud, have a distinctive sound, and are small enough for the cramped mounting areas of most cars. They do draw a fair amount of current, particularly among the louder types, but most are under 2 amps. A bell is an excellent choice for any system, particularly for interim duty while you accumulate cash for a high-power siren.

Most bells are designed for fire warning systems in buildings, and instead of this being a drawback, it's quite an advantage. Most of these bells are designed for outdoor use, and must meet very strict standards for durability and noise level, and these standards are set and monitored by fire marshals—a notoriously tough group. If a given piece of equipment is said to meet either California or New York fire standards, you know it's a strong piece of work. What this all comes down to is that there's a large number of bells available that can stand the tough environment under your hood and with their noise levels reliably determined and marked right on them.

Bells (Fig. 8-8) are available in 3, 6, 8, 10, and 12-inch diameter sizes, 6, 12, and 24-volt power requirements, and sound levels up to 115 decibels and more. Their one fault is that a steady sound of any kind tends to fade away against background noise. The already excellent characteristics of a bell can be enhanced by the addition of a modulator. In fact, a high-power bell with a modulator ranks a close second to a high-power siren, and at one-quarter to one-third the cost: you can buy a really high-power bell for $30 or so. One more advantage of bells is that they are a self-breaking circuit, and thus can be used with a simple thyristor power switch or modulator.

Sirens are of course the standard noisemaker for most security systems. They are available in a bewildering variety of sizes, shapes, loudnesses, and prices (Fig. 8-9). Good, loud units will make your wallet cry for mercy, but the cheap ones (the bulk of the market) aren't worth the effort of bending over to pick up from the shelf. The advantage of sirens over the other types of noisemakers is that

Fig. 8-8. Bells are an excellent alarm output device for automotive security use. They are best when used with a long-period (2-3 second) modulator to break up the steady sound. These are 10- and 12-inch models; others are available down to 3 inches.

they are instantly and universally recognized as alarm signals. They draw immediate attention from everyone, police and passersby alike.

Most of the sirens on the market use the so-called "European police" sound, an alternating set of high and low tones. The American rise-fall type is not as common, since most are mechanical and require a switching circuit to cause the tone to rise and fall. They are also the most-prohibited type, since they could be confused with authentic emergency vehicles.

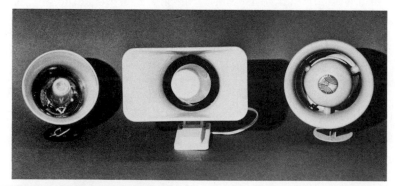

Fig. 8-9. Sirens are the epitome of alarm output devices. Cheap ones aren't worth the money and the good ones will run you quite a bit. If you have to have a siren, spend the money and get a good model. Otherwise, use a horn or bell.

The European type is super, provided that it has sufficient power and a sharp division between the two tones. The cheap, low-power types give off a sort of "weeble-weeble" sound that vanishes in 100 feet. The better units have two loud, clear sounds and a sharp interchange between them. If you want the best you can get, you may end up using two differently-toned horns and an alternating power switch.

Evaluate sirens carefully before making your purchase, and don't forget to examine the option of building your own from scratch. If you want to save the heavy outlay of cash that an off-the-shelf high-power siren calls for, you may want to build your own. It isn't simple, but it's worth it in the sense that it gives you more flexibility in the sound and design of the unit.

Since it is difficult to build amplifiers that will run off of 12 volts and give more than 4 or 5 watts, it is better to stay with commercially-built amplifiers. There is a whole class of amps almost custom-made for automotive security use: auto-stereo power boosters.

If you use a power booster, you will have to build the input circuitry for it. Most units require a 4- or 5-watt input signal for maximum output, but some slightly up-market units can accept a line-level input of roughly 200 millivolts.

The noise-generating circuits of Figs. 7-6 and 7-7 are excellent places to begin for designing your own input circuitry. Develop whatever sound pleases you, and then use the output circuitry of Fig. 8-10 A and B to hook it ot the power amp.

Essentially, you want to buy the cheapest amplifier you can find that delivers the kind of power that you want. The more expensive units only give better sound, and that's not necessary for siren use. You may have to run your input drive a bit below maximum to cut the worst of the distortion, but most boosters will easily deliver 85-90 percent of their rated power at 10 percent or less total harmonic distortion—which is lousy for music but fine for sirens.

Stereo power booster's outputs cannot be summed together directly to drive a single output speaker, and most attempts to do so will destroy the unit. If the unit comes with a schematic, you or a reliable stereo dealer should be able to figure out a way to drive a single load without burning out the unit's output stage. You may just end up driving two separate speakers.

The output of your hand-built unit will be difficult to interface with the outside world, as weatherproof speakers that can handle anything over 5 to 8 watts are expensive. The types that are designed

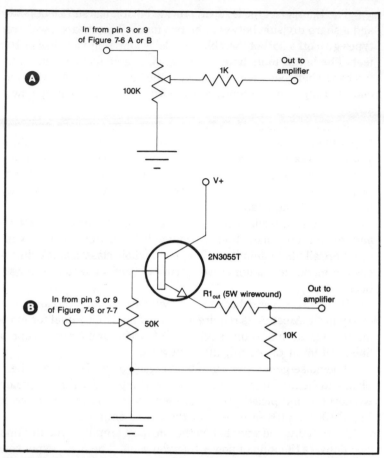

Fig. 8-10. These two circuits are used to tie the noise-generating circuitry of Fig. 7-6 or 7-7 to a stereo power amplifier's inputs. Figure 8-10A is used to turn the 555/556's output into 200mV signal needed for line-level input types and 8-10B is used to generate a 5-watt signal for the others. The output resistor in Fig. 8-10B should be a 5 watt wirewound unit. The pot in both should be used to adjust the gain to a level that gives a maximum output without too much distortion.

especially for high power and behind-the-grill mounting can run over $100.

The only cheap option you have is to build a weatherproof box and mount the necessary one or two 6 × 9 speakers inside. Again, you would use the cheapest speakers you could find to handle the power, not expensive items such as Jensen Tri-Axials. The speakers would be mounted in the box, with their edges caulked, and their fronts and backs, cones and frames alike, sprayed with a silicone sealer. This shortcut method will work, but the speakers will not last more than a year or so. Still, it's cheaper to replace the speakers even two or three times at $20 a crack than it is to lay out a hundred or more for the specially designed unit.

A really sophisticated type of audible alarm output, briefly mentioned in Chapter 7, is a synthesized-voice output. The recent drops in the cost and complexity of voice-synthesis technology (a voice synthesizer can now be built with two or three ICs and for less than $50, and costs are still coming down) make it a viable alternative to simple noise warnings.

Voice synthesis is still too complex to go into detail here; furthermore, there are several different approaches and techniques. However, if you are willing to work with a particular type, you can find schematics for simple voice synthesis circuits in nearly any recent issue of any electronics magazine. The low-power-output circuits described there would be used to drive a power booster, as described above, for a shattering effect—on thieves. Someone yelling "STOP THIEF!" at the top of his electronic lungs in a concrete parking garage is a virtually guaranteed way to protect your car. And there are some more inventive phrases you could use.

Visual Alarms

There are more than a few problems with audible alarm devices, but the first and foremost problem is that even the loudest and most distinctive type tends to get lost in a crowded parking lot or garage. I once tried to trace a siren in a large parking garage and stumbled across the car purely by accident, and then had to put my ear to the grille to make sure that I had really found it. It is difficult to tell where a sound is coming from in any large space or "concrete canyon," or even to tell what direction the sound is coming from.

The solution is to give the vehicle a visual alarm output in addition to its noisemaking one. Flashing lights are the simplest and most effective visual alarm signal. I don't recommend that you add any lights specifically for security system use, since that would involve unnecessary expense and may be illegal in some areas. Instead, there are two types of lights found on all road-going vehicles that are not only easy to use, but also legal: the headlights and the emergency four-way flashers. Most states specifically allow a vehicle's security system to flash any and all regular-equipment lights as a warning, even if flashing lights on vehicles are otherwise prohibited.

Adding the vehicle's four-way flashers to the alarm output is so simple that no security system should do without them. Some vehicles use a simple thermal flasher element to pulse the lights on and off, and in those cases a simple thyristor power switch can be used. In most cases, though, since the four-ways are intended to operate over a wide voltage range, a separate nichrome wire is used to heat the bimetallic strip to cause the flashing. This type of load would be continuous, and a thyristor would never unlatch. So, a relay or heavy-duty transistor type power switch should be used for four-way flasher duty. Be sure to add the incoming power lead on the far side of the normal flasher on-off switch.

The second visual flashing-light output, the headlights, is more complicated but effective in situations where the car may be left in a large open area or a ways away from people (such as a large construction site or a park). Since the headlights draw a comparatively large amount of current, a heavy-duty relay type modulator must be used. Since headlights take a moment to come up to full brightness and another moment to die away, the flash period of the modulator should be fairly long—about four to five seconds or so. Also, be sure to figure the large draw of the headlights into the design of your backup power supply, or, to save money, you can power them directly from the main battery and just accept the risk that they may be rendered inoperative in the event that the thief cuts the battery cables.

Since headlights are only visible from half or less of the vehicle's circumference, it would be a good idea to use the four-way flasher as a secondary visual alarm. An excellent idea would be to have a switch to select either headlights and four-ways, or four-ways alone.

Radio Pagers

One of the most effective additions to an automotive security system's output is a radio pager (see Fig. 8-11). These complicated devices consist of a transmitter with 1/2 to four watts of power in the vehicle, and a small doctor-type pager that you carry in your pocket, briefcase, or purse. When the system goes into the alarm state, the transmitter is triggered and sends a signal to the pager, alerting you that there's trouble.

The pagers are available under a number of brand names and from a variety of sources, but most are manufactured by Page Alert Systems. They use the CB radio band and transmit coded tone groups, so someone else's unit won't trip your pager. It used to be that the higher-power units were quite expensive, but they are now

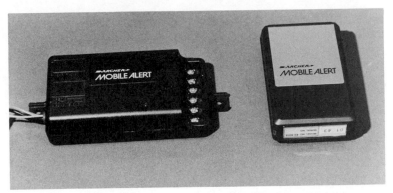

Fig. 8-11. A radio pager is an extremely effective type of alarm output device. When the alarm state is reached, the transmitter (left) sends a coded signal to the pocket receiver, which then beeps a warning and alerts you to take action. This is a 1/2-watt transmitting power unit; units with up to 4 watts are available. This is a Radio Shack unit.

available for about $100. The 1/2-watt units can be found for about $75. The smaller units share the vehicle's radio antenna, and the higher-power ones use a separate CB antenna. If your vehicle uses a disappearing antenna, or if you want maximum range from the smaller unit, use a separate CB antenna as well. You don't need a quarter-wave whip for either type; a roof or trunk mounted "shorty" will do an excellent job.

Most pagers are designed for use as complete security systems, a practice I can't agree with. As an add-on alarm output, pagers are superb, but as complete systems, they edge into the gimmick class. The gimmick class is loaded with security systems that take one complete, excellent idea and then build an inferior system around it. Throw away the sensors and doo-dads that come with the pager and use just the transmitter and pocket receiver.

Some modification will be needed for most pager units, since they are designed for underdash mounting and have controls and such on them. It should not be too difficult to set the controls at the necessary settings, add a remote-on circuit—connected to the arming output of the mainbox—and then hide the whole thing as you would any other module.

Pagers don't require a CB license. This requirement has been rescinded by the FCC recently.

DISABLING DEVICES

The final type of alarm output device really isn't an alarm device per se. Disablers are modules that render the vehicle undriveable during and after an alarm state. They are the final wave of defense against the auto thief. They will not stop a smash-and-grabber or a stripper, but they will prevent a thief from driving the car away.

When designing and installing disablers, be absolutely certain that they themselves are completely disabled when the vehicle is running, so that they cannot cut in while driving. A sudden loss of power could cause an accident.

The basic operation of a disabler is simple. When the security system goes into the alarm state, the alarm output signal is used to latch the disabler module in its open state. When open, the disabler interrupts a critical vehicle system's power supply. The actual sequence of events will vary with each vehicle, installation, and interrupted system, but essentially the vehicle will not start or will not remain running. The disabler will remain latched open until the security system is properly reset.

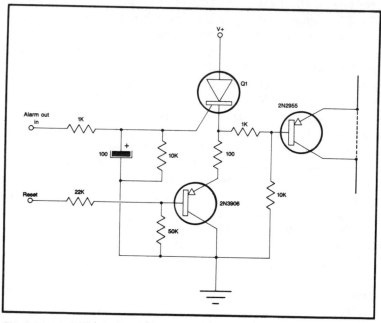

Fig. 8-12. An SCR-based disabler is one way to disable a low-power circuit. The hot lead of the item to be disabled is represented by the line XX. Normally, the circuit will be completed by the output transistor. When the security system goes into the alarm state, the SCR will latch the transistor's base high and cut the circuit until a high reset pulse (from disarming) is received at the reset terminal. Even with a high-power transistor such as the 2N2955 shown, this disabler should not interrupt more than a 2-amp line.

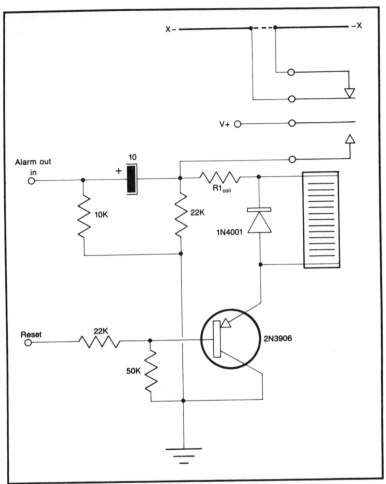

Fig. 8-13. The DPDT relay-based disabler can interrupt a 10-amp or more current source. Its operation is identical to the SCR type's otherwise. The relay must draw a minimum of current to keep from running the battery down.

A disabler is basically a relay with a simple drive circuit that takes the alarm output signal and uses it to latch the relay open. A second signal—usually the arming output signal from the mainbox—is used to unlatch the relay. The relay can be the ordinary electromechanical type, or a semiconductor switch.

The semiconductor type (Fig. 8-12) is limited to interrupting at most a 1- or 2-amp source. A light-duty SCR is used as the latching element, and its output is used to drive a heavy-duty transistor that actually interrupts the current flow to the vehicle system. The transistor must be heavily heatsinked, and the entire disabler module must be very close to the interrupted power line. Any wires running to or from the existing power supply line must be the same or larger gauge.

The relay type disabler (Fig. 8-13) is somewhat more flexible, since it can interrupt more power—up to ten amps—and is more positive in its operation. Its drawback is that even the best relay draws some current to hold itself latched, and it may draw that current for some time before the system is reset. Since a relay-type is almost the only type that can be used in some situations, be sure to use a relay that draws the absolute minimum coil current.

The operation of the relay type disabler is much the same as that of a relay-type mainbox. One set of contacts of a DPDT relay is used to latch the relay on after triggering, and the other is used to open the power supply lead of the interrupted system. An input buffer circuit is used to keep the load on the alarm output low, and another simple transistor switch is used to unlatch the relay when the proper reset signal is received.

Both types of disabler draw a certain amount of power, and the unavoidable problem is that of battery draining. There are two ways to prevent the disabler in your system from draining the battery excessively.

First, if you do not drive the car at least once a day, you should make it a point to check it out at least once a day. The addition of an alert indicator and a low-battery indicator, as discussed in Chapter 7, would make the job of checking much easier.

Second, you can equip the disabler with a long-period reset timer, with a reset period of one to two hours. A simple 555-type timer will not be adequate for this use—use one of the other ICs specifically designed for long-period use, such as Exar's 2240 and 2242. With such a timer, the vehicle will be effectively disabled for a long enough time to discourage even a determined thief, but will still reset before causing any appreciable battery drain. It should be overridable by the proper reset signal (i.e., disarming). This is the better choice, since it does not require daily monitoring of the system. Such a reset timer is a required addition to any truly first-class system.

When designing and constructing the disabler, be sure to give it excellent bypassing. If it is ever called into duty, it may have to suffer some wild supply spikes and drops as a thief tries to cut it out or tries to hotwire the car.

Also, be sure that the relay or transistor is capable of handling the current of the line that they are interrupting—and a large derating factor wouldn't hurt. Make the device fail-safe, so that if it does not receive power or a disable signal, the system it interrupts will still function. It is not difficult to make either type simply fail to operate in the absence of power.

Starter-Relay Disabling

Probably the most elementary use of a disabler is to cut out the starter relay. The starter itself, of course, cannot be directly cut out, but interrupting the current to the starter relay is just as effective. This is also the safest way to utilize a disabler, since even if it totally malfunctions it cannot interrupt a running engine.

The disabler should be mounted in a protected, hidden location. The best place would be under the dash. The starter lead can be interrupted anywhere between the ignition switch and the point where it disappears into the wiring harness. If you build the module small enough, it could even be hidden inside the steering column shroud—in most late-model cars, there is a large amount of open space between the actual steering column and the outside plastic shroud. By mounting the disabler inside the passenger compartment instead of under the hood, it can be protected both physically and by the security system itself.

When the disabler is latched open, the starter relay will not engage and the engine will not start. This, however, is the easiest type of disabling to defeat, since a thief could use a short piece of wire to jump the starter relay closed, bypassing the ignition switch and the disabler.

Ignition Disabling

Using a disabler to cut out a vehicle's ignition is an excellent way to foil a thief. By interrupting the power supply to the ignition system, the thief can crank the engine until the battery is dead, and it won't start. Some thieves will give up at that point, thinking the vehicle defective, but many will realize that the vehicle is being disabled. Very careful installation of an ignition disabler is called for to foil such a determined thief.

Since the unit will have to go under the hood, the way to hide is to make it appear to be a regular part of the car's electrics. There are two ways to do this. First, locate an inoperative "black box" from a wrecked vehicle made by the same manufacturer as your own. Dismantle it carefully and discard the interior guts, and then use the case to house your disabler. This trick is most effective if the case has the manufacturer's logo cast or stamped into it. Don't make it too pretty—you want it to look like it's been right there since the car was new.

Another way to disguise the unit is to mount it in an ordinary aluminum or steel case and then paint it a greasy flat black. Add an identifying sticker or decal, and a thief will never spot it. The sticker can be peeled off of another component in your car, or from a wrecked vehicle. What you want is not a clean, shiny FORD or MOPAR logo from the speed shop, but a grungy, smeared one that reads "FOMOCO part #ZZ645A9311" or some such.

The installation and operation of an ignition disabler is not difficult. For standard, nonelectronic ignition systems, the disabler can be used to interrupt either of the primary wires to the coil or to the distributor. Electronic ignitions are a little more complicated. In general, you want to disable the ignition system's control box, but care must be used in the method used. If you are not thoroughly familiar with the system in your car, ask a reputable mechanic—preferably a factory-trained one—which lead can be safely interrupted without the possibility of damaging the ignition system. Don't guess! Ignition systems get more complicated every year, and picking what seems to be the proper lead may turn the control box into a smoking ruin.

Fuel Pump Disabling

If your vehicle is equipped with an electric fuel pump, you can use a disabler to cut its power supply. This is probably the most effective way to use a disabler, since few thieves would realize that it is a security system in operation when the car stumbles and dies after running for a few minutes. Even if he does suspect it, a fuel-pump disabler can be made virtually impossible to find.

Most electric fuel pumps are near the fuel tank, although a few may be found under the hood. The pump's power lead can be interrupted at any point. A few places where the disabler may be mounted are under the rear seat, behind an interior rear-seat trim panel, or in the trunk. If possible, it should not be mounted anywhere near the fuel pump. If it must be out in the open at all, use the disguise techniques described for the ignition disabler.

In operation, the fuel pump disabler will allow the engine to start and run, but it will die in less than a minute and will not restart. With luck, the thief will have gotten to an embarrassing point (an intersection, a parking tollbooth, or the street) when the vehicle dies. He will have to abandon it and run.

The uses of a disabler are another security system design point that is only limited by your imagination. Any electrical system can theoretically be disabled by a security system. What about disabling a vehicle's fuel injection system, for example? When installing disablers, just be sure that their operation won't damage any part of the vehicle.

9

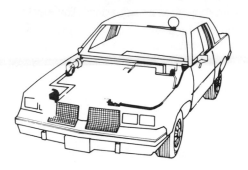

A Complete System

BECAUSE THE PURPOSE OF THIS BOOK IS NOT TO TELL YOU how to build a particular security system, but rather how to design and build a unique, custom system that fits your specific needs, this is a rather unusual chapter. Its purpose is to tell you how to take the segments of information from the previous chapters and put it together to design your perfect system.

Chapters 4 through 8 each presented all of the facets of design of a particular *subsystem* of an automotive security system. It is now time to pull all of this information together and design a complete security system.

MINIMUM REQUIREMENTS

There is no limit to how sophisticated and complex a security system can be, but at the other end of the spectrum, there are limitations on how simple it can be and still be a complete system. How each of the required minimums is met is not important, as long as it is met. Once you understand the minimums, the maximums are only limited by your imagination.

Mainbox

All security systems must have some sort of central switching element: The mainbox. Chapter 5 explained how the mainbox must have a trigger input, an arming input, and an alarm output. When the arming input is in the armed state and a brief or continuous low-level is received at the trigger input, the alarm output will latch into the high state.

Beyond this basic operation, anything can be added to the mainbox—entry and exit delays, reset timers, deadman controls, etc.

Input

To trigger the mainbox, the system must have at least one input—in other words, one sensor. That sensor's output must remain high or unconnected until it senses tampering or an unauthorized entry. At that point, its output should drop to a low level, either momentarily or until the tampering or unauthorized entry is over.

As mentioned in Chapter 6, a single type of sensor or sensing is completely contrary to all common sense design rules. A single sensor is absolutely required for system operation, but more than one is required for proper system operation.

Output

A security system requires at least one output of one type or another. The most common is an alarm device that generates an audible or visible signal; nearly all systems will have this type of output. Other systems may use a disabling device that renders the vehicle undrivable, or a radio-paging device to alert the owner even when he's miles away, and most systems will use several types at once.

MODULAR DESIGN

This entire book is written around a modular design type of system, which is the most effective way to design any complex device that must be adapted to many different applications. It is the only approach that makes sense for automotive security system design.

The advantages of the modular component design system are numerous. Essentially, the security system is broken into a number of *building blocks* that can be strung together in any configuration. This allows a number of tricks that would be impossible with a non-modular design:

■ Installation is simplified, since it is easier to mount and hide a number of small modules than it is to place one or two large ones.

■ The sensitivity is greater, and the system is more effective, since each component and sub-component can be mounted where it can best do its job, without compromising the placement of any other component.

■ It will be much more difficult for a thief to disable the system if it is a half-dozen or more modules scattered throughout the vehicle. He may be able to cut out a few of the components, but it will be almost impossible for him to get them all.

■ Perhaps the best advantage of the modular system is that each component can be duplicated or omitted as required by your own needs.

■ The final advantage is that the modular design system allows you to build a large, complex, expensive system in easy stages. You can start with a basic system and gradually add to it until you fulfill your wildest dreams—without straining your time or your budget.

With all of this working for you, why use any other design system?

Modular Component Designing

The first stage in using the modular component system is to draft out a design sheet. There are a series of steps to work through, and at the end, you have a sheet that contains your complete system design. From that, you can build your system.

The first step is to decide exactly what you need to protect your vehicle. Look at the vehicle you are designing the system for—what about it do you want to protect from theft or vandalism? Door, hood, and trunk/hatch sensors are pretty much required, as are a motion and a vibration sensor. From there, it's up to you what else you want protected—ski racks, tool carriers, gas caps, whatever.

Once you have decided what it is that you feel needs protection, you have to examine the protection options that fill those protection needs. There are usually at least two ways to accomplish any given protection, and all it should take is a persual of the proper chapter in this book to make your choice. If you don't find it there, you should at least find a suggestion about where else you can look. A look through any good security company's catalog (such as Louisville Lock & Key or Mountain West) should give you an idea of what's available off the shelf.

Beyond the options that are required, you will want to examine options that you may want. In this category would be the choice of arming control, and whether or not to use a specialized input-conditioning circuit, a sensitivity selector, a backup power supply, and the like. It's best to throw in at this stage everything that you might want to add on later, since a particular module that you will want to add may require a slightly different design for another module—most likely the mainbox. It's easier to add a little bit to the "first wave" system components in anticipation of modules to come than it is to rip those modules out later and modify them.

After you've chosen everything that you want to be a part of your system, the next step is to list the modules that will be needed. Some may be straight from the pages of this book, some may be modifications of those, and some may be ones that you completely design yourself. List the ones that are taken directly from here, and sketch out the schematics for the modified and new ones. I suggest you bench test every circuit and system on a solderless breadboard using the actual components that you will use in the system before actually constructing and installing the modules. An error in design or component selection is a lot easier to catch on your workbench than it is in the vehicle. Be certain to measure things like the module's current draw as well.

After that, you must sketch a hookup diagram. Simply draw each module in a logical area on a large enough sheet of paper, and then draw in each connection that will be needed. Use pencil and keep rearranging things so that you end up with a neat, workable diagram. Draw in each module in black, and neatly label each wire and terminal shown. When that is finished, you will need to mark the wiring requirements on the hookup diagram. The easiest way to do that is to trace each wiring line on the sheet with a colored felt pen, using a different color for each gauge or type of wire.

You now have a basic design sheet to work from.

INTERFACING

Interfacing the various components of a security system should not be a problem, particularly if you've built them all yourself. Sometimes, though, modules may need help to understand each other, most often if a user-built module must work with an off-the-shelf device. In these cases, there is a whole group of circuits designed specifically to translate one module's signals into those that another can understand.

Interfacing User-Built Components

There are two simple rules-of-thumb to keep in mind when interfacing components that you construct. First, there should not be any protocol problems—all of that should be taken care of by the design of the components themselves. All components taken directly from this book will work together without problems. Any that you design yourself must conform to the standard input and output protocols described in the appropriate section of the book.

Second, all system components should use the same source voltage. If half of the components use the vehicle's system voltage and half require 5 volts, you will just be multiplying your design problems. If a particular component or subcomponent requires an odd voltage, use an on-card regulator to supply it.

Interfacing Commercially-Built Components

Essentially, interfacing an off-the-shelf component is the same as interfacing one that you build yourself. You want to make it fit your system, not vice versa. If you have to, use the translation circuitry described next. A better solution, if you can use it, is to modify the component to work correctly.

Translation Circuitry

The circuits shown in Figs. 9-1 through 9-3 can be universally used to translate one type or level of signal to another. They will probably find at least limited use in almost every system, no matter how careful your design work.

Inverters turn a high level to a low one, and vice versa. An inverter for interfacing use can be unidirectional or bidirectional in its operation. A unidirectional inverter will only actively invert one level into another, and not vice versa. A bidirectional inverter will actively invert both high and low levels. The inverters of Fig. 9-1 can be made either unidirectional or bidirectional by changing the values of $R1_{high}$ and $R1_{low}$ around. The inverter in 9-1A is primarily for use in high-current, high output/low-current, low output situations; the low resistor should be a fairly substantial value and the high one as low a value as necessary. The inverter in 9-1B is the opposite, characterized for use in high-current, low output/low-current, high output situations; its low resistor should be a low value and its high resistor as high a value as possible. In all cases, the transistor used should have adequate current capacity to handle the load. The 2N3906 and 2N2222 shown can handle up to 300 milliamps. For very low-power inversion, the 4049B CMOS inverter may be used.

Voltage limiters and boosters change one voltage level signal in-

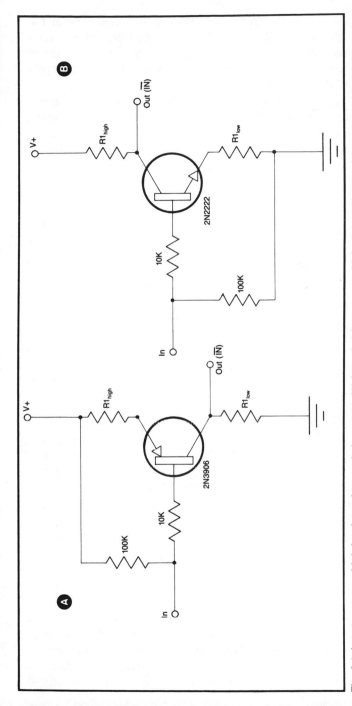

Fig. 9-1. Inverters turn a high level to a low, and vice versa. (A) Intended for use as a high-current high-level/low-level/low-current low-level sourcing device, so R1$_{high}$ should be low-valued and R1$_{low}$ should be fairly high. (B) Intended for high-current low-level/low-current high-level sourcing, so its high resistor should be high in value and its low resistor low. Both types can be used alternately or for both high- and low-level high-current sourcing, if necessary.

179

to another voltage level either higher or lower than itself. The voltage limiter in Fig. 9-2A will, when it receives the higher voltage at its input, respond with the lower voltage at its output. The lower voltage would be set by the zener diode. The voltage booster in 9-2B works in the opposite way, taking a lower voltage and responding with a higher one. The high voltage in this type would be limited to the system supply voltage unless you are willing to fool around with dc-dc converters.

Protocol translators are the most complex form of translation circuitry. They turn one type of signal into another—a low or high level into a pulse or frequency, or a frequency into a high or low level, or something even more complex. The simple differentiator of Fig. 6-12 could be used in situations other than input conditioning, and is thus one type of protocol translator.

The *frequency-to-pulse/level converter* is perhaps the most difficult of the types discussed here. It is not practical to present even a sample of designs for this type of circuit, due to the enormous number of variations that might be useful in an automotive security system; however, a description of the basics of their operation is certainly in order.

Essentially, you want a circuit that will wait for a given input frequency, with a given amount of bandpass or slack in its accuracy that will give a set output response when that frequency is detected. Therefore, there are two parts to this type of circuit: a bandpass filter and an output circuit.

A bandpass filter is a selective filtering array that only lets a given range of frequencies pass through it, sharply attenuating any frequencies above or below that range. The degree of attenuation and the width of the bandpass are almost infinitely variable, depending upon the exact filter design and the component values used. In general, an active filter using an op amp is preferable to a passive filter using only resistors and capacitors and such.

The output circuitry, which would be designed to give whatever type of output the next stage of the system required (a high or low level, a single pulse of either polarity, or even a different frequency), would sense the presence of this filtered frequency and give off its response.

There is a single integrated circuit that performs precisely these functions: the LM567 tone decoder. It is simple to use, reasonably accurate, and quite cheap. However, it has two sharp drawbacks. First, it requires a 6—9 volt power supply, meaning that in order to use it in most vehicles, a lower-voltage power supply must be add-

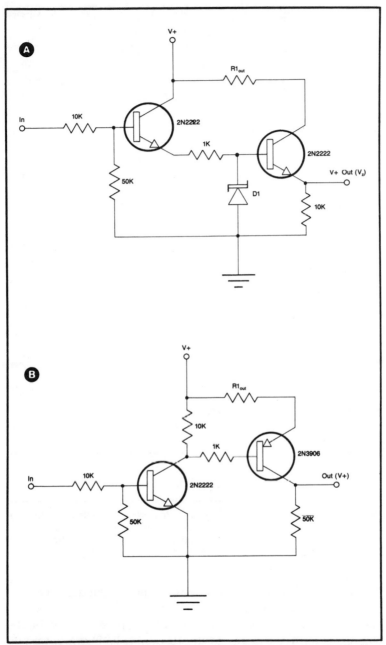

Fig. 9-2. (A) This voltage limiting circuit will remain low as long as its input remains low, and go high—to V_z—when its output goes high. (B) This voltage booster will go high—to V+—when its input goes higher than about 1/4 V+.

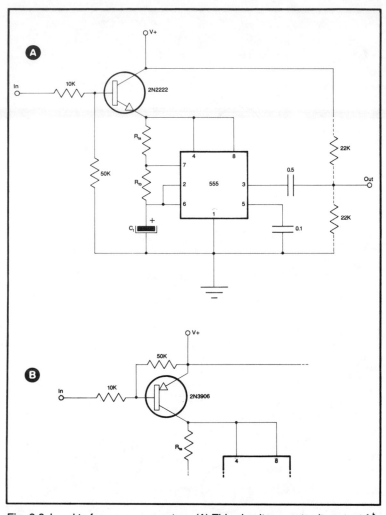

Fig. 9-3. Level-to-frequency converters. (A) This circuit generates its output frequency when its input goes high. (B) Generates its output frequency when its input goes low. The output frequency of both types is determined by the 555's timing components. The output can be held high or low as its off state, depending on which pull resistor is used.

ed, meaning additional cost, complexity, and current draw. The last point, incidentally, brings us to the 567's other shortcoming, excessive current draw: some 10—15 milliamps are required by the chip. A search of the more obscure IC catalog listings may turn up a low-power version of the 567, or even an altogether different chip that performs the same functions with a lower current requirement.

The alternative is to design the whole circuit using discrete components—difficult, yes—but made easier by the appearance of a new IC. This CMOS IC (carried by Radio Shack) is a group of several programmable filters; it draws a minimum of current, needs a minimum of external components, and has a maximum of flexibility and accuracy. If your system really needs a frequency-to-level converter, this chip or one of its family would be a good starting point.

The level-to-frequency converters are much simpler and probably have a wider use. Figure 9-3A shows a converter that will produce a frequency when its input is high; Fig. 9-3B will produce a frequency when its input is low. For both designs, the output frequency is set by the timing elements of the 555 timer IC, and the output can be normally (off-state) high or low, depending on whether a pull-up or a pull-down resistor is used after the output capacitor. Do not use both.

EXAMPLE SYSTEMS

Although I intended that you use this book to design a system to fit your own needs, it is still appropriate to present some complete example systems, for two reasons. First, there are certain to be some readers that would rather simply follow a diagram than take the trouble to design one from the ground up. (Nothing wrong with that.) Second, even if you intend to design your own, having a few complete systems to look at may be a great help to you. These four systems represent three levels of complexity, from very simple to moderately complex. They are certainly not carved in stone; feel free to make changes in them to suit your own needs. For example, the vehicle-horn alarm on the first one could easily be replaced with a siren, the pager could be deleted on the fourth, and so on.

Simple Relay

The simple relay security system shown in Fig. 9-4 is about as basic as a system can get. It is too simple for all but the lowest-risk vehicles.

The mainbox is the simple-relay type of Fig. 5-2. Pinswitch sensors on all doors, the hood, and the trunk lid are used, as well as a motion sensor. The motion sensor would have to be set fairly low, to avoid excessive falsing. An outside keyswitch is used for arming control.

The sole output device is the vehicle's existing horn(s), driven

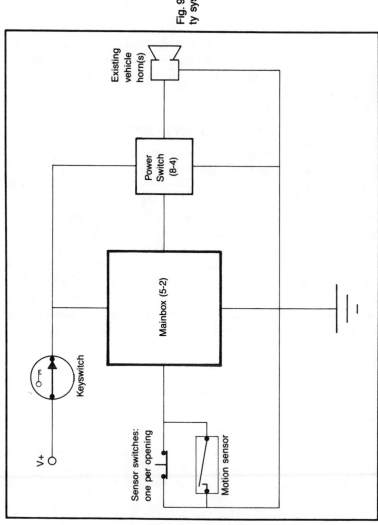

Fig. 9-4. A simple relay-based security system.

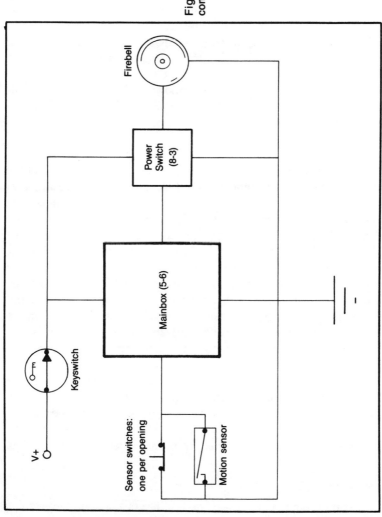

Fig. 9-5. A simple discrete-component security system.

through the simple relay power switch of Fig. 8-4. Note the existing horn wire is left in place; if other than the relay-type power switch is used, a heavy-duty diode should be placed in each line feeding power to the horn to prevent feedback problems. The relay-type power switch, of course, is an open circuit when off, and no current can feed either direction through it; no diodes are needed.

Discrete Component

The SCR-based system shown in Fig. 9-5, using the SCR mainbox of Fig. 5-6 is a somewhat more advanced system than the relay type above. It is also armed with an outside keyswitch and uses door and hatch pinswitches along with a motion sensor as well. It drives a bell as an alarm output through the SCR power switch of Fig. 8-3. If an alarm output device other than a bell is used, make sure that it will work with an SCR power switch.

Both this system and the one above could easily add the unijunction reset timer of Fig. 5-4, and in fact, this modification is highly recommended.

Low-Power IC

The low-power IC type mainbox in Fig. 9-6 is built around the CMOS NOR-gate mainbox from Fig. 5-8. As you recall, this 4001-based mainbox draws around 3 microamperes of standby current, and thus can remain armed for months without appreciably draining the battery's charge. Because it, like the previous two systems, does not have entry and exit delays, the keyswitch must be on the outside of the vehicle. The change here is that the keyswitch is connected to the mainbox via the deadman control circuit of Fig. 5-11. Even if a thief uses a dent-puller to yank the keyswitch from the fender or quarter panel, the system will remain armed or arm itself. The primary advantage of this system is that it incorporates a reset timer, so that it will shut off the alarm after five minutes or so.

The sensors used are all door and hatch lid pinswitches, a motion sensor, and a vibration sensor. Again, both the motion and vibration sensors should be set fairly low in sensitivity to keep the number of falses down. The output devices are a siren and the vehicle's four-way flashers, both powered via the buffered relay power switches of Fig. 8-5.

Advanced IC

The system in Fig. 9-7 is loaded—it has one of almost everything

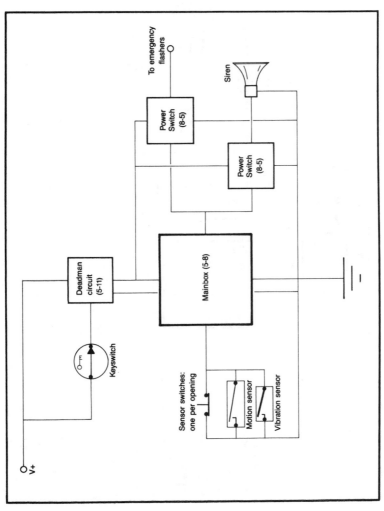

Fig. 9-6. A 4001 CMOS IC-based security system.

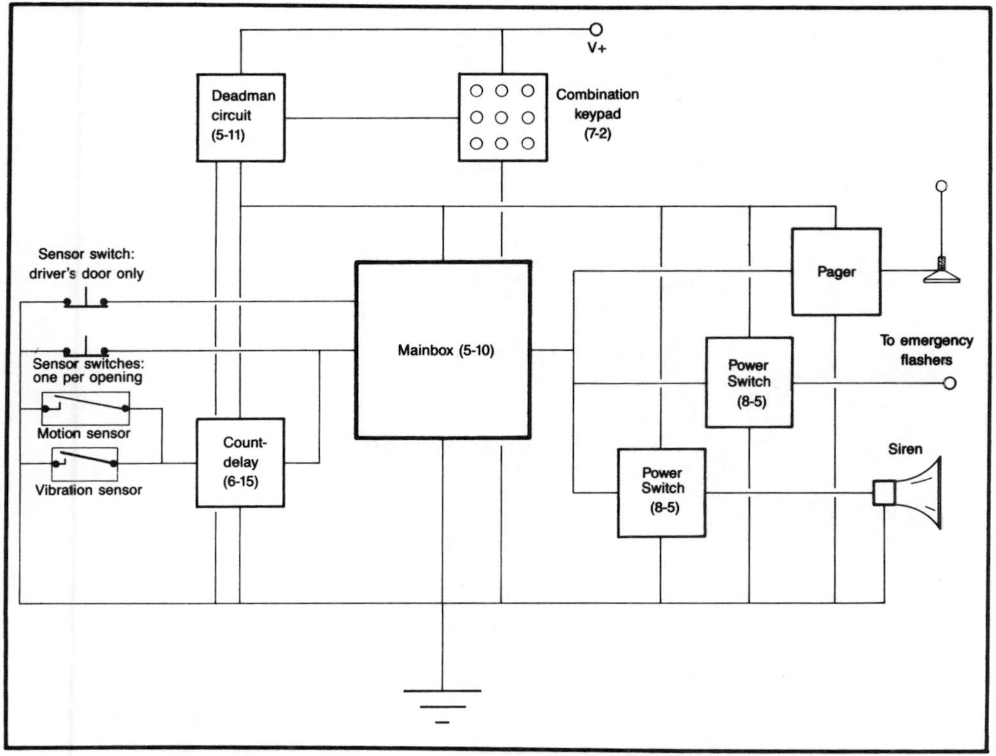

Fig. 9-7. A full-featured security system with entry, exit, and reset delays.

in its design. However, it could still be added to! Not shown, for example, are a backup power supply, a collision sensor, or indicators. The door's pinswitches could be replaced by magnetic or IR types.

Its heart is the 555/556 mainbox of Fig. 5-10, which incorporates entry, exit, and reset timers. Its arming control is on the interior of the vehicle, of course, and is the combination keypad of Fig. 7-2, which controls the system via the deadman control circuit from Fig. 5-11. It has one pinswitch that goes to its delayed trigger input from the driver's side door, and all other door and hatch lid pinswitches are connected to its direct trigger input.

It also uses a motion and a vibration sensor, whose outputs are routed through the count-delay circuit of Fig. 6-15 to the direct trigger input. Its output is triple-threat: two buffered relay power switches driving the four-way flashers and a siren, and a radio pager.

These four examples cover almost all of the bases for the security system designer. Again, you can change, add to, and revise all four to better suit your needs, or just come up with one of your own.

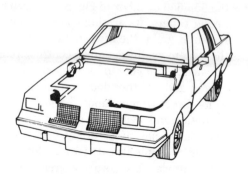

10

Installation

T HE FINAL STAGE IN BUILDING AN AUTOMOTIVE SECURITY system, and one that is much taken for granted in both home-built and commercial systems, is installation. This chapter is equally applicable to systems that you build and systems that you buy. By this stage, both types are a collection of little black boxes, anyway.

Most commercially-built systems, as has already been mentioned, are severely compromised in order to make their installation easier. This does not mean that they are easier to install properly. Even with the gross simplifications made in most off-the-shelf systems, there is still a right and a wrong way to install them.

Of course, it is not possible to detail every phase of installing a vehicular security system, because of the endless numbers of both systems and vehicles. What is presented here, then, is a group of very specific guidelines that can be applied to almost every installation. Nearly all of the focus in this book is on security for road-going vehicles—cars, trucks, vans, etc. If you are installing a security system in another type of vehicle, such as a motorcycle, boat, or small plane, then you will have to use your own knowledge, experience, and common sense to get you through the unusual situations that are sure to crop up. One note: if you are installing a system in a light plane, use great care during all phases of construction and installation, and be certain that you follow all applicable rules and regulations. There are few things more closely regulated than small aircraft.

FUNDAMENTALS

The basics of installing an automotive security system are quite straightforward and closely related—but not the same—as those involved in installing an auto stereo system. The tools and techniques are quite similar, but the objectives are very different.

Objectives

There are four basic objectives to keep in mind when planning and executing a security system installation. The first and foremost one is that the system must be installed to give absolute maximum security and coverage.

This objective covers a lot of ground. A properly installed system will not only give the maximum security it can to a vehicle, but also to a large extent protect itself as well. The main technique for accomplishing self-protection is to use entry and exit delays and an interior arming control. If these are used, along with some care towards mounting the rest of the system's modules in protected locations, a thief will not be able to even try to disable the system without tripping it.

All components have a best location where they can do their job the most effectively. Find that best spot and use it. For example, sensors should be mounted where they are the most effective—pinswitches must be mounted along the frame of the door or hatch, of course, but there is a best spot somewhere on that frame, most likely away from the hinges. Motion sensors, to give another example, should be mounted towards the end of the vehicle's centerline, where the shaking and rocking motions of an entry attempt would be amplified.

The second objective is to minimize the disruption of the vehicle's normal functions. The security system's parts and controls should not interfere with existing components of the car or truck. This includes appearance: disfiguring a vehicle disrupts its function almost as much as if there were some mechanical interference. It also includes comfort: if you keep banging your knee on a keyswitch or snagging your clothes on a protruding pinswitch, you aren't going to be very happy with the system.

Third, the security system must be installed with an eye to reliability. While much of a system's reliability is tied up in its design and construction, the importance of proper installation should not be overlooked. Modules must be firmly mounted so that they cannot work loose; wires should be properly supported and protected so that they do not fray against edges or break under strain; controls must be mounted so that years of use will not loosen or damage them.

The final objective in installing your system is to ensure that it's easy to maintain and use. The controls and indicators should be easy to see and reach, even if hidden or disguised, and all components should be accessible for repair and maintenance. The last does not mean that they shouldn't be protected, of course, but the module should be accessible with a little bit of work—such as removing the rear seat or pulling an access panel.

Tools

The tools needed for installation need not be expensive or hard to find. For a single installation, the more specialized ones can be dispensed with and their job done with a simpler tool. For a really top-notch installation, though, or for more than one, the specialized tools will really pay off in terms of speed and precision.

A basic mechanic's tool kit is the first thing required—a set of wrenches and sockets that fit your car, along with a few pairs of pliers, a pair of vicegrips, and a full set of screwdrivers. Tools to make some jobs easier would be a set of hollow-shaft nutdrivers, a ratchet screwdriver such as Stanley's "Screwball," or even a power screwdriver. (You will end up pulling and resetting dozens of screws in the course of an installation, and a ratchet or power screwdriver will really speed things up. If you are going to be doing more than one installation, be sure to buy or borrow one of the two.)

One point you should note is that many cars, particularly later models, use at least one oddball type of screw or bolt. A very common type is the Torx-head screw, which has a six-pointed star inset in the head, much like an Allen-head. Torx tips for ratchet drivers or Torx drivers can be picked up at any good parts store. A set of Allen wrenches, by the way, will be necessary for many vehicles.

In addition to the mechanical tools, there are a number of electronics tools that will be needed. If you are going to use lugs and rings to connect the modules together, you will need an assortment of sizes and a crimping tool. These tools usually have a number of functions built into them—wirestripping, wirecutting, bolt cutting, small-terminal crimping, large-terminal crimping, etc.—which makes them a good buy even though a good one will run you about $20. If you are on a really tight budget, you can use channel-lock pliers or vicegrips to crimp terminals, but this isn't really recommended.

If you are going to solder the wiring to the modules, you will need a small soldering iron and some medium-gauge solder. A gun-type soldering tool is recommended because it has an on-off trigger; a pencil-type could be mislaid and cause a burn or even a fire. An excellent tool for this type of work is a cordless soldering iron, such as those made by Wahl, because they have an on-off switch, heat and cool rapidly, and are free of dangling cords. They are fairly expensive, though, and are not necessary unless you are going to be doing a large number of installations.

A continuity tester or alarm installer's box is a very useful device to have. The latter is a special test unit that will perform a number of checks peculiar to an alarm installer's job. They are sold under a variety of strange names, such as "Peter's Meter" and "The Little Black Box." For one or two installations, though, a simple continuity tester can be cobbled up from a handful of workbench parts.

Both tools can be replaced by a cheap VOM, such as Radio Shack's $10 unit. Don't drag your $200 Fluke or Simpson out into the garage or driveway with you. The meter is going to get dropped, kicked, banged around, and the like, and it'll hurt less with a $10 unit. The cheapie will work just as well for the light-duty job of installation double-checking.

An electric drill with a set of bits is required. A variable speed-reversing type would be the best, even if you have to borrow one. A dimpling punch to give the drill a starting place in a panel is absolutely required.

For holes that are larger than a drill can make or are oddly shaped, there are two types of tools. A hole-cutting punch is a punch and die set that are bolted together through a small drill hole, and then tightened together, cutting a neat hole in the panel between them. They are very fast and neat, but their use requires a different punch and die set for each size and shape of hole. A basic set starts at about $50, with each additional die set running about twelve or so. If you are going to be doing a lot of installation work, they will be worth the money, but for one or two jobs they aren't worth it. A cheaper and more flexible option is a tool called a nibbler; a toothed device that starts in a 1/4-inch drill hole and then chews out any size or shape of hole you need. They are only about $20 for a good model, but are much slower than the punch and die set. They have no limitation, however, on the size of the shape of the hole they cut.

An electrician's fish tape would be nice to have to pull wires through long narrow channels; you might be able to pick up a ten or fifteen foot broken section from an electrical contractor. Along with that, a sharp razor knife, such as an X-Acto, and a supply of blades would be a good idea.

Procedures

There are several universal procedures that apply to automotive security system installations, but one that is absolutely inviolate is to disconnect the vehicle's battery ground connection before starting work. The tremendous current stored in the battery could start a fire if you short even a small power lead, and the potential for damage to the vehicle's electrical systems—the security system included—is high. Pull the cable each and every time you work on the security system.

At some point in the installation, you are going to have to drill a hole in a metal or plastic panel. Since you are going to be using a plastic or rubber grommet to protect the wire or wires from chafing and to seal the hole, the hole must be drilled to fit the grommet.

The first step in drilling a hole, after selecting the spot, is to make sure that both sides of the panel at that point are free of wires, hoses, components and the like. To prevent unnecessary damage, always make a starting dimple for the drill to start its work in. The dimple will keep the bit from skittering around and marking the surface up. A punch must be used to dimple a metal surface, and a razor knife will work on plastic. A single-speed drill can be used, but a variable-speed type is usually a good idea. Do not use anything other than a variable-speed type in finely finished surfaces such as turned aluminum or walnut.

If a larger hole than a drill is needed, a nibbler or a punch-and-die set must be used. The punch and die will make a very neat cut, as already mentioned, but they are very expensive. The nibbler is the cheaper and more flexible tool. A nibbler requires a 1/4-inch drill hole to start its cut in, and from there it's a matter of nibbling away at the edges of the hole until it is the desired size and shape. Again, make sure that both sides of the panel are free of obstructions before you start to cut.

With drilling and cutting, it's best to follow the old carpenter's axiom, "measure twice, cut once." Look the job over before even plugging a tool in—don't just plunge in and hope for the best.

You are almost certainly going to have to route wires through almost every part of the car. Many times, you can avoid pulling panels and trim pieces if you are willing to use a little patience instead. An electrician's fish tape or a reasonable substitute can be pushed through a cramped, twisty passage and used to pull a wire back through. It's a tricky job, but it will work and it's worth the trouble to be able to avoid pulling yet another part of the interior.

AUTOMOTIVE CONSTRUCTION

Most older cars, particularly nonluxury types, are put together in a pretty straightforward manner. The screws or bolts that hold a panel or a piece of trim in place will be either exposed or just hidden by a lip. As cars get smaller, more sophisticated, and more expensive, the technology holding them together gets more complicated. Snap-together parts, special fasteners, adhesives, and one-way clips are getting more and more common. If you have to do any disassembly of your interior at all, you are almost certain to run into at least some of these.

The snap-together parts can usually be popped off and back on without any problem. You might have to spread the fastening vanes or wings to get a proper fit. The glued-on parts can be peeled off and then reattached with contact cement after the mating surfaces are cleaned; use a water-based contact cement for plastic parts, since the acetone-based type might cause damage. In some cases, where parts do not fit together closely, a thicker, mastic type adhesive may be needed. A good auto-parts store should stock several types of automotive adhesives.

Special fasteners fall into two groups, reusable and nonreusable. Most types of spring clips and all types of screws and bolts are almost infinitely reusable, although items such as Tinnerman or speed nuts are not. Barrel clips, the small barrel shaped fasteners that hold trim on by its integral studs, are another non-reusable type. Again, a good auto-parts store or the vehicle's dealer should stock replacements.

COMPONENT PLACEMENT

The first step in installing an automotive security system is finding a place in the vehicle for the components of the system. Most types of components will have their locations destined by their function and your design, but some may have considerable latitude in their placement possibilities.

The way to start is by assembling all of the system's components in one place, from the sensors to the mainbox. Take each one and go through the vehicle until you find the best mounting place possible. It's best to make a sketch or keep a list as you go along, to keep everything straight. It's also easiest if you take the components in logical order—start with the mainbox, then the input-conditioning modules, then the power switches, the alarm components, and the sensors. It's usually best to leave the sensors until last, since they are the trickiest of all to install properly.

The first rule to use in locating a component's mounting place is that it must be placed where it best serves its function, and the second is that its location must be protected from tampering. The latter will usually mean that a component must be mounted inside the passenger compartment or perhaps in the trunk—anywhere where the module is inside the security system's sphere of protection.

As for the first rule, every component really does have a "best" location. For a component such as a mainbox, an input circuitry module, or an arming-control circuitry module, you will want a very secure place such as under the rear seat, behind an access panel or kick panel, or inside (not under) the dashboard. These places should only be used if the component can only be accessed by using a screwdriver or wrench.

A backup power supply must be mounted very securely as well, but its size and heft compared to an all-electronic module makes for some problems. Perhaps the best location is on the inside of the firewall, at the transmission hump; second choice would be in the trunk or spare tire well.

Noncritical modules, such as indicator controls, can be mounted anywhere out of sight.

The placement and mounting of controls and indicators was covered in depth in Chapter 7.

Direct sensors must go at the hatch or door that they protect, or anywhere along an electrical line that they watch, obviously, but as was briefly mentioned above, there is an ideal spot somewhere along the line or doorframe. For a brakelight sensor, for example, the sensor package could be placed either at one of the brakelights, or at the brakelight switch (usually near the master cylinder). A door sensor will usually be on the door side away from the hinges, so that even the slightest opening of the door will close the sensor. Courtesy lights are the exception, but they are carefully designed and matched to the vehicle so that they close as soon as the door is ajar.

If your system has audio listening devices (of the direct sensor type), then you will have a special problem. You have to first decide what it is you want them to listen for. In most cases, it will be the opening of a door; there is then a choice of placing it near the hinges or the latch. If your vehicle's latches make a lot of noise (I don't mean a squeak or a grating sound, but just a good, decisive click or clunk), then your best move might be to place the sensors there, so that the first move of a thief's entry attempt will close the sensor. If the latches are fairly quiet, a better move would then be to put the sensor near the hinges. In both cases, you would want the actual listening component of the module to be right at the hinge or latch. You may be able to find a location on the backside of the member that they are bolted to by removing a trim panel. If the listener is to be used for another purpose, these same guidelines should give you an idea of the effect you're trying to accomplish.

Remote sensors have a great deal of latitude in their mounting locations. Motion sensors, as mentioned, should go towards the end of the vehicle, where the rocking motions are amplified, and their long dimension should be parallel to the vehicle's centerline. A second choice would be on the firewall, but this would mean mounting it off-center as well; towards the very end is definitely better.

Vibration sensors have somewhat limited areas of coverage, so if a single unit is used, it must be located where shocks from an entry attempt will be felt. There are three such places: the doors, the hood, and the trunk or hatch lid. The doors are the foremost place for vibration sensor use. Hoods and trunks are only candidates for vibration sensors in an absolutely all-out system: since they will have pinswitch-type sensors, the only advantage that adding vibration sensors would give would be to stop entry attempts, as opposed to actual entry. This is a thin line of reasoning, though, because strippers and auto burglars do not pussyfoot around—they slam the crowbar in and break the latch in a fraction of a second, so that it would be a race between the pinswitch and the vibration sensor to trigger the alarm.

If you do decide to use hood and/or trunk vibration sensors, then mount them on the latch assembly itself, out of the way of striking components, set their sensitivity fairly low (when a jolt comes, it'll be a hefty one), and do not route its lead through a count-delay module, but instead directly to the direct trigger input of the main-box. The approximate sensitivity can be set by adjusting them so that they close when you strike the latch area from the outside as hard as you can with a gloved hand. Don't dent the car or yourself!

The door-type use of a vibration sensor is a better way to use this type of sensing. The sensor must be mounted so that it can sense small jolts and shocks from both or all four doors. Doors are different from hoods and trunks in that a thief will spend a considerable amount of time with tools to open the door with minimum damage. This can be used to the designer's advantage by sensing this tampering and tripping the alarm prior to entry and perhaps even prior to any damage.

There are two ways to mount vibration sensors to protect doors. The first is to use a single sensor mounted either between the seats (under the parking brake housing or console) so that jolts from both doors would trip it. This is adequate for some systems, but the sensor's sensitivity must be set high and it must be used with a count-delay input conditioner.

A better way would be to use a single vibration sensor for each door. This would mean only one additional sensor, so even for fairly low-budget installations, this is the better option. The sensors should be mounted behind the door latches, in the quarter panel of two-doors and the B-pillar of four-doors. The sensitivity should be set so that a hard rap with a knuckle on the door lock closes the sensor's contacts, and a count-delay circuit would be a good idea. For a two-door car, then, the doors would be protected against both entry (by the pinswitches) and entry attempts. A four-door's front doors would be highly protected, and its rear doors would be somewhat protected as well. Four separate vibration sensors are not really necessary, since most entry attempts will be through the front doors.

In all cases, the vibration sensor must be mounted to a strong structural member of the vehicle, so that the shocks and jolts of entry attempts are transmitted to the sensor. Any plastic or padding of any sort between the shock and the sensor will tend to filter out the shock. (As an alternative to mounting the sensor between the front seats, you could mount it in the roof on a support member behind the headliner.)

If any components must be mounted underhood, the primary thing to keep in mind is that they must be only accessible by raising the hood, and the hood should only be openable by either unlocking it or by an interior latch handle. The components should be on the top of the fender apron, or blocked from underneath by engine or engine-bay parts—preferable large, hot, or greasy ones. The best way to protect underhood components is to disguise them, as discussed in Chapter 8. Components that cannot be disguised, such as sirens or bells, should be painted a dull flat gray or black, so that they cannot be readily spotted. For some reason, these parts always come in a bright red or chrome finish. Get rid of it! Ideally, these components should be mounted in an armored box, but underhood space will almost always prevent this. One thing that can be done with them all is to hide and cover their wiring so that it cannot be tampered with easily.

By the way, if you do not use a backup power supply—or even if you do—you might consider armoring the battery cables. Use two lengths of flexible BX conduit, from an electrical supply store, along with the necessary fiber bushings and end fittings. If the cables are covered end-to-end with this material and its ends bolted to the frame and the battery support, a thief will be unable to cut them and almost unable to pull them loose. Be certain to use the fiber bushings on the BX's ends, as the sharp edges could cut through the cable—with disastrous effects. It would not be a bad idea to heavily grease the inside of the BX, to prevent chafing, and to check the cables' conditions regularly. Be certain as well that the positive cable's armor cannot touch either end terminal.

All components mounted underhood or in the trunk must be sealed tightly, to keep out moisture, dust, dirt, and oil. They should also be temperature-protected: keep them away from exhaust and cooling components.

COMPONENT MOUNTING

All components, no matter what type, must be firmly mounted to their selected location. There are a number of ways to attach components.

Most off-the-shelf components have mounting provisions built in—screw ears or holes, or threaded bodies and the like. Any components you build yourself must have mounting provisions added.

The best way to mount all components, and the only way to mount those that are heavy or subjected to heavy vibration, is with bolts, nuts, and lockwashers. This would apply to items such as backup power supplies, sirens, bells, pager transmitters, and the like. The bolts should be further secured by the application of a locking compound such as Loctite. Bolts are probably the best way to mount all components, regardless of weight.

For lighter-weight components, large sheet-metal screws can be used, again with lockwashers to hold them in place. Make sure that the screw does not protrude into a finished panel on the other side, and if it protrudes outside the vehicle, be sure to caulk the hole with a silicone-based caulk to prevent leakage and rust. The screws used should be galvanized, and their length chosen to give about 1/4 inch of thread on the far side, after passing through the component and the mounting surface. Always use a small pilot hole—about half the thread diameter—to start sheet-metal screws.

Straps are a good way to mount lighter components. Use the big, heavy wire ties with the steel fibers running through them; they can be found in lengths from 6 to 18 inches and can be chained together to form longer pieces. They should be run through loops or holes on the component, and around a sturdy support in the vehicle. At least two, in a crossing pattern, should be used for maximum security. The straps are cheap, fast to put on, and can be quickly cut and replaced for service access.

A fourth way to mount components is with adhesives. There are a number of types of adhesives that can be used in an automotive environment—contact cement, superglue, "liquid rubber," silicone sealer, and other heavy mastic-type glues. If used at all, they should be used in generous amounts and only to support lightweight components. Be certain to follow the directions for each type very carefully, particularly paying attention to the one point that they will all have: "parts to be joined must be clean and dry . . ."

WIRING

Wiring a security system's components together will call for at least a couple of different gauges of wire, along with several types of terminals and fittings. It's best to have more than you need of each item—particularly wire—so that you won't run out or have to take shortcuts. Do each wiring job properly—you've come too far to skimp now.

One advantage (a slim one) of off-the-shelf systems is that they very often come with a pre-made wiring harness, with the appropriate gauges and types of wire fitted to a connector that pops onto the mainbox. As can be imagined, this is a great time saver, but it has almost no application for the home system designer. (If you are doing more than one system, you might consider measuring and estimating wire lengths and constructing as many harnesses as needed.)

Wire

There are three types of wire used in automotive security system installation: solid, stranded, and multiconductor. The last is of course not a fixed type of wire, but rather a subtype. The most common use of multiconductor wire will be in those situations where a number of small conductors have to be routed from one point to another, such as between the keypad and the electronics of the combination lock of Chapter 7. There are two different types of multiconductor wire: ribbon cable and telephone wire. The first type, often seen in computers, is a large number of very small conductors (typically 28-40 gauge) bonded side-by-side in a common plastic case. Types with six to forty or more conductors are commonly available. They can usually be split for fewer-conductor needs. The other type, telephone cable, has three to eight heavier gauge conductors inside a tubular plastic sheath. This type would be called for when higher current must be carried.

The choice between solid and stranded wire is up to you, but in general, stranded wire is easier to work with (more flexible and easier to solder) and solid is easier to shape (where a wire must hold a bend or corner, or example).

The gauge of the wire is more critical. Table 10-1 should be used as a guide to sizes for given current loads.

Any even slightly experienced electronics hobbyist will recognize that these figures are extremely conservative; there are wires commonly available with maximum current capacities as much as 6 to 10 times these figures. However, for common plastic-insulated wire, these figures should be used, in keeping with the policy of heavy derating in automotive security system design.

Connectors

There is an endless variety of wire terminals, lugs, and accessories available, as even a quick look through an electrical sup-

Table 10-1. Wire Sizes for Given Current Loads.

Wire Gauge (AWG)	Maximum Current Capacity
8	20.0
10	12.0
12	8.0
14	4.0
16	2.5
18	1.75
20	1.0
22	0.75
24	0.45
26	0.25
28	0.15
30	0.075

ply or auto parts store will show. The most common types are ring and spade lugs, used to terminate wires for connection to screw terminals; splices and taps, used to make quick, strong connections to existing wires; and multiple connectors in X (four sockets) and Y (three sockets) configurations. These last are used to join several wires together in common. More specialized types abound; just check through an electrical catalog or store. An example is the multiple-conductor connector, of which there are so many types it would be impossible to list them. As with so many other automotive security components, a little searching will turn up just the type you need.

There are two types of terminals: crimp-on and solder-on. Although the crimp-on type requires a special crimping tool (and thus an initial investment of $10 or so), it is generally superior to the solder-on type since soldering a large number of items inside the body of a car is a difficult task at best. The solder-ons are superior to the crimp-ons in one respect: they are totally vibration-proof. The crimp-ons can come loose with time. (A properly crimped terminal is almost as vibration-proof as a soldered one, but the difference between proper and improper can sometimes be a very fine line, and only one terminal has to fail to render the system inoperative. In general, the crimped type is the better bet; a crimping tool can't burn a hole in your seats!)

Beyond the wire and the wire terminals, there are a number of accessories that can make a job much easier or neater. Wire ties are one of the most common; these are small nylon straps that have a built-in locking buckle and are used to tie off wires to support points. A selection of sizes from 4 to 6 inches will come in handy. Another useful item is spiral wrap, a type of plastic tubing that has a continuous spiral cut in it. It comes in a variety of sizes and can be used to bundle wires together after the wiring is complete. It allows wires to enter and leave the bundle at any point along its length as well.

Procedures

The first step in wiring the security system up, after all of the components and such are mounted, is to sketch out a component guide that shows where each component is, and then draw in each wire that must be run (for convenience, multiconductor cables can be shown by a single line). Each different type of wire should be identified using a different color of felt pen.

A color-coding system for the wires themselves is also a good idea—for example, all power wires red, all sensor wires blue, all control wires yellow, etc. Any color system can be used as long as you note down its specifics in the system's documentation. This will simplify hookup, and, later on, testing and repair. A really involved system isn't usually necessary, but at least the elementary types of wire should be distinguished.

Routing the wires from place to place should not be difficult; most cars have numerous wiring runs and you can usually just poke the wires through the same holes and supports. Some common places to find runs are above the doors (behind the headliner or trim), under the doorsills (very common), and along the transmission hump. One interesting advantage to paralleling the existing wiring is that even the most inquisitive thief or service person will not be able to trace the system's components.

All of the wiring should be routed inside the vehicle's passenger compartment; none, if possible, should be outside. The exception will be what little wiring must go under the hood, and it should be located as far from tampering as possible (along the edges of the hood line is a good place), particularly with an inside hood latch or a secondary hood lock.

All of the wires should be properly supported: if they do not lay snugly in a recess, they should be tied off to a sturdy point at short intervals. In some cases, where small motions may be present across a gap that a wire must bridge, a small amount of slack can be left to prevent breakage.

Getting the wiring through surfaces is one of the trickiest parts of wiring a system. Most surfaces will have at least one opening—for other wires, for ventilation, or for another reason. If the surface you have to get through does not have any openings, you'll have to drill or cut your own. (See the section on cutting and drilling above.) Be certain to use grommets or other insulators at all points where the wire crosses a panel or edge to prevent chafing damage, and use a good-quality silicone sealer to caulk all holes to keep out dust, water, and air drafts.

11

Operation and Maintenance

O NCE YOUR SYSTEM IS DESIGNED, BUILT, AND INSTALLED, ALL that is left for you to do is to use it. That's not as simple as it might sound—there are right and wrong ways to use a security system. Wrong use is usually not using the system when you should.

Using the system is all that remains—unless it malfunctions. In that case, you will have to find and repair the malfunctioning module. About the only good thing about repairing the system is that no one knows more about its design than you!

USING YOUR SYSTEM

There are several facets to using a vehicular security system, none of which should be prohibitively complicated. Once again, it's all a matter of common sense.

Documentation

It is absolutely mandatory that you keep copies of all of the system's documentation, for several reasons. First, if you need to repair the system, or if you want to modify it, you will need the various schematics and wiring diagrams to help you remember exactly what and where everything is. Second, if you ever sell the vehicle, the new owner will want to know all of the applicable information so that he can use and repair the system. Third, you may impress someone with the system so much that they want a copy for their car!

The documentation need not be exhaustively complete, but you should have at lease the following items:

■ The schematics for each component, whether directly taken from this book, modified, or purely your own design. A neat sketch is all that's needed; make sure that all modifications and part designations are marked. It wouldn't hurt to add adjustment points and voltages and other data to the schematics, for future reference.

■ The accompanying literature and specifications for any off-the-shelf hardware in the system, as well as sketches of any modifications made. If you use the purchased module without modification, be sure to save sales receipts and other items that will be needed for a warranty repair. If you modify the unit, particularly inside its case, you are just about certain to void any warranties, but save the material anyway, just in case.

■ The system wiring diagram.

■ The component placement diagram. (It's embarrassing to forget where you put the disabler or power switch.)

Once you have nice, neat copies of all of the above, and anything else that may be applicable to your system, place them in a manila envelope and put it in a safe place—like a safe deposit box.

A neat thing to have, particularly if your system is very sophisticated, is a usage card. This is a small card, kept in the vehicle, that briefly explains the operation of your system. A short recap of delay times, switch operation, sensitivity options, and the like will be a help both to you and to borrowers of the vehicle. Simply type all of the information on a small piece of index card and have a photo shop laminate it for durability, and then keep it in the glove or console compartment. One thing not to list on it: key ID numbers or combination codes.

Maximizing Security

There are a number of simple steps that you can take to maximize the system's effectiveness and in turn the vehicle's security. First of all, don't discuss the system in detail with anyone—even friends. The existence of the system need not be a secret, of course, but there is no need for anyone besides you to know its details and specific capabilities.

It the system is not an automatically-arming one, be certain to use it every time the vehicle is left—even in your own driveway or garage, and especially when it's only left for "just a minute!" If you don't use it, even once, you risk losing the vehicle, and all of your work will be for nothing.

A sticky problem—no pun intended—is deciding whether or not to use window decals, like those in Fig. 11-1, that warn that the vehicle is protected by an electronic security system. Most police and security system manufacturers recommend them, but there are two sides to the issue. It all depends on whether you want to use the system as a deterrent or as a warning device. The use of the stickers will deter most joyriders, vandals, auto burglars, and amateur thieves, and they will leave or go on to the next car without a second thought. On the other hand, if a professional thief knows that the system is there, he can make very careful moves and defeat it. If a pro has no indication that the vehicle is equipped with a security system, he will almost certainly trip it on his first attempt, and you can take steps to ensure that there are no subsequent attempts. One rule of thumb might be that if you are trying to protect your car primarily against the lower orders of criminal, use warning decals, and if your vehicle is of even remote interest to a pro, do not use them.

Also, to maximize the security of your vehicle, use all of the applicable mechanical protection methods that you can—if your wheels are expensive or otherwise likely to attract a thief's attention, use locking lugs; if your car has vent windows, use clip-locks, and so on. Even the best electronic system can use a little mechanical

Fig. 11-1. Window warning stickers are heavily promoted by police and security system manufacturers, but may or may not be a good idea. See text.

help to give you the most security it can.

Finally, remember that an electronic system—no matter how sophisticated—is not a replacement for good old common sense. An electronic system should be regarded as a backup, a last wall of defense against automotive crime, and not as an infallible, impenetrable guard against all evils. The pointers given in the first chapter about parking and locking your vehicle safely should always be kept in mind.

RESPONDING TO AN ALARM

What do you do when your security system sounds the alarm? The first rule of responding to an alarm is the hardest to get across: don't play hero. Never, never confront thieves or strippers or try to apprehend them. The most you should ever do is make a lot of noise on your approach to the vehicle to scare them off. Automotive criminals do not as a rule carry weapons, but any criminal caught in the act and cornered is likely to be dangerous.

To reiterate: don't act like John Wayne. Your car is not worth it!

If your alarm goes off, even if it appears to be a false alarm, you should consider moving the car to another, safer location. If the alarm was tripped by a professional, he may return to try his luck again, this time prepared to defeat the alarm. You should also keep a much closer than usual eye on the car for the next week or so as well—a clever pro will follow the car around, waiting for an opening. If your caution continues, he's bound to get discouraged and look for a new target.

There are two basic types of alarms: noise and silent pager. Each demands a little different approach in response. There is one thing that applies to both types: use extraordinary caution at all times.

Noise Alarms

When responding to a noise-type alarm, the primary thing to keep in mind is that you should let the alarm do its job. Let the siren and the flashing lights chase the thief away; they can't be bashed on the head like you can.

The best approach is to move to a location where you can see the car from a distance—at least 100 feet or so—and just keep an eye on the car until the alarm resets. If you are in a garage or a shopping center, consider getting a security guard to go with you to the car—that's what they're there for! If a guard is with you, you don't need to wait for the alarm to time out. In other locations, you might want to consider flagging down a cop to escort you—once again, that's what they're there for.

Once the alarm times out and you have determined that the area is clear, go ahead and move the car to a safer location.

Silent (Pager) Alarms

With a silent alarm, you should consider immediately calling a security guard or cop to go to the vehicle's location. If you must respond yourself, do not go alone. Use extreme caution—the thief will not know that you're coming and could be surprised into violent action.

If the car is in a dark area—do not respond yourself. In that case, call the police first. If the car is in a well-lit area, or a well-populated one or both, you can respond, but still use a great deal of caution.

MAINTENANCE

You may sometime have to dig in and repair your security system; even the best-designed, best-built, and best-installed system will develop a problem now and then. It need not be a traumatic experience. If you built and installed it, you can repair it as well. If you have kept good documentation, as discussed earlier in the chapter, finding and repairing a problem should be easy.

Testing

Even if the system never gives you a minute's trouble, you should give it a thorough test regularly—at least once a month. Take the vehicle to a reasonably deserted area where the noise won't bother anyone to perform the test.

Arm the system, and then test each sensor by opening the door or whatever it takes to trip it. When the alarm goes off, reset it and go on to the next sensor. If any sensor is on a delayed trigger input, time the length of the delay to make sure it's within spec. When you test the last sensor, let the system complete its alarm cycle: if it's equipped with a reset timer, let it time out; if it's not, just let it run for a few moments (to see if there are any overheating or other problems) before resetting the system.

If the system is equipped with any oddball circuitry or components, test them as well.

208

Troubleshooting

Troubleshooting a malfunctioning security system is not difficult. You should have your documentation to guide you, and all that it takes is a little systematic work.

Use logic to trace down a problem. If the entire system is inoperative, don't start by checking the sensors. The problem would more likely lie in the power distribution or backup power supply modules, or in the arming control, or lastly, in the mainbox.

If the system has too many false alarms, there is most likely a problem in the sensor array, or possibly in the mainbox.

If part of the alarm output does not work, check the output device first, and then its power switch, and then its wiring back to the mainbox. If all of the alarm output is dead, then the problem would most likely be with the mainbox's alarm output signal.

If the arming control works intermittently, the problem is most likely within the control itself—whether it be automatic, keyswitch, or keypad in type.

These examples are obviously pretty general, but they illustrate the point. Troubleshooting a security system is like troubleshooting any other electronic device—it's just that there aren't any manuals to guide you.

Repair

Once you have found the defective part of the system, you can repair or replace it. Usually, major components can be repaired, but be sure to test them thoroughly before returning them to duty. If the failure was not caused by physical damage—such as an accident—then find and fix the cause of the problem before using the system again.

Be sure to check the wiring that connected the module into the rest of the system for damage, such as scraped or burned insulation. If any is found, or if the original problem found was damaged wiring, it is best to replace the entire length of wire instead of splicing it. If splicing is the only option, be sure to use a strong soldered joint and cover it with a tight wrap of electrical tape.

If you spend very much time away from home, it might be a good idea to carry a repair kit for the security system. It would be awful to have the system fail while on a long trip and not be able to keep your car—and luggage and the like—safe.

Since you should carry a basic tool kit anyway, you should have the simpler tools such as wrenches and screwdrivers with you. Some of the tools that you might need and would not carry as part of a regular car's tool kit are a dc soldering iron, solder, spare wire of the gauges that you use in the security system, a pair of needlenose/sidecutters, and a pair of wire strippers. With those, you should be able to make most simple repairs to your system.

You will need spare parts as well, but only you will be able to make up a list of exactly what parts you should have. A well-stocked repair kit would include one of each type of IC, transistor, and semiconductor used in the system, as well as a couple of each type of capacitor and resistor. Beyond that, it's up to your discretion. With any luck, you'll have done a good enough job on the system that you'll never need the repair parts.

Appendices

Appendices

Appendix A

Automotive Security Suppliers

T HERE ARE SEVERAL COMPANIES THAT SUPPLY SPECIALIZED
components for use in automotive security systems, as well
as regular electronic components and complete security systems.
This listing is not intended to be complete, but should give you a
guide to what's available and where. No endorsement of any company on this list is intended or implied.

Active Electronics
P.O. Box 1035
Framingham, MA 01701

*Extremely large inventory of all types of
electronic components, cases, and the
like.*

Burbank Enterprises
950-D N. Rengstorff Avenue
Mountain View, CA 94043
[415] 968-9099

*Manufacturers of the Audio Safe,
among other automotive security
products.*

**Chapman Industries
Corporation**
2638 United Lane
Elk Grove Village, IL 60007

*Manufacturers of a high-quality line of
automotive security systems.*

Digi-Key Corporation
Hiway 32 South
P.O. Box 677
Thief River Falls, MN 56701

*Large inventory of prime electronics com-
ponents, excellent volume discount.*

Heath Company
Benton Harbor, MI 49022

Suppliers of the Heathkit line, which includes high-powered sirens, sonar interior guards, pagers, and other kit-form items.

Incognito Manufacturing Works
881 Richmond Avenue
San Jose, CA 95128

Manufacturers of the Stereo Disguise.

Jameco Electronics
1355 Shoreway Boulevard
Belmont, CA 94002

Large line of electronic components and kits. Some unusual items. Interesting catalog.

Louisville Lock & Key
3926C Shelbyville Road
Louisville, KY 40207
[502] 896-0456

Stocks a huge variety of automotive security systems and equipment; catalog a must as a source of ideas.

Mountain West Security Equipment Distributors
4215 N. 16th Street
P.O. Box 10780
Phoenix, AZ 85064
[602] 263-8831

Suppliers of extensive range of security hardware.

Techne Electronics Limited
916 Commercial Street
Palo Alto, CA 94303
[415] 856-8646

Manufacturers of the Ungo Box line of automotive security systems.

Appendix B
555 Timers

THE 555-SERIES MONOLITHIC TIMER ICs ARE PRECISE, FLEX-
ible, inexpensive timing devices perfect for use in automotive
security systems. They are insensitive to voltage change, can use
a wide variety of supply voltages, and can have timing periods from
milliseconds to hours.

The basic design for the entire series is the 555. It is a single
timer usually supplied on an 8-pin DIP. Its close-coupled sibling is
the 556 dual timer, which is the equivalent of two 555s on a single
14-pin DIP, with shared V+ and ground connections. A somewhat
different relative is the 558 quad timer, which has four timers in
a single 16-pin DIP. Its V+, ground, reset, and control voltage pins
are common for all four timers, limiting their flexibility, and they
can be used for monostable operation only.

The above group of timer ICs are inexpensive, but their power
consumption could be excessive for other than short-period use in
an automotive security system context. There are two groups of low-
power-consumption 555 derivatives.

The first derivative type is the 7555/7556 CMOS timer ICs.
They are identical pin-for-pin to the 555/556, but are constructed
using CMOS technology. Their primary advantage is extremely low
power consumption (about 80 microamperes during standby for the
7555). Their actual operating characteristics are slightly different
than the 555, and circuits using them must usually be slightly adjusted for proper operation. They are supposed to be completely

static-proofed, but cautious handling is still recommended.

The second derivative group is the L555/L556 low-power bipolar timer ICs. Once again, their main advantage is low-power operation, in this case about 0.5 milliamps standby current for the L555. They are virtually identical to the 555 and 556, being made up from conventional bipolar-transistor design. The major change in design is the comparator resistor divider string; in the 555, it is made up of 5K resistors, and in the L555, of 45K units. The comparators themselves are also modified slightly for lower power draw.

All three types operate in much the same way. The only major difference in operation is the varying levels of output current: the 555 can source and sink up to 300 milliamps; the 7555, 150; the L555, about 200. Refer to the individual manufacturer's spec sheets for exact figures.

The 555 will be used as the example for the rest of Appendix B. The pins of the 555 IC are as follows:

#1: Ground. Should always be tied directly to the circuit ground bus.

#2: Trigger. Must normally be held high. The falling edge of a pulse that drops below the 1/3V+ level will trigger the IC into its timing state.

#3: Output. Will normally be low from power-up on, until a trigger pulse is received; it will then go high for the duration of the timing cycle.

#4: Reset. Should normally be tied to the circuit V+ bus. When brought low, will force output low (in both monostable and astable modes), end the timing cycle (for monostable operation), and hold the timer disabled and the output low until it is returned high.

#5: Control Voltage. Directly connected to the upper comparator's divider string input. Normally not used, it should be tied off to ground via a 0.01 to 1 microfarad capacitor to stabilize the IC. A voltage applied here can be used to change the timer's built-in timing coefficient of 1.1.

#6: Threshold. Should be connected to the timing R/C junction. Will normally be clamped to ground by pin 7 until the timing cycle is initiated; the capacitor will then begin to charge via the resistor until its charge reaches the 2/3V+ level, which will end the timing cycle. The capacitor will then be clamped to ground again.

#7: Discharge. Connected to pin 6 for monostable operation. When the IC is in its nontriggered state, the Discharge pin is grounded, holding the timing capacitor uncharged. When the timing cycle begins, it floats in a high-impedance state to allow the capacitor to charge. When the timing cycle ends, it again clamps the capacitor to ground.

#8: V+. Should be connected directly to the circuit's V+ bus. V+ can be from 5 to 15 volts, and slightly lower for the 7555.

The 555 timer can be used in one of two modes: monostable (one-shot) or astable (free-running). The monostable mode is used for period timing, and the astable mode is used to generate a square-wave frequency. The former has the most use in automotive security, with the latter being restricted mostly to sound generation.

In monostable operation (Fig. B-1A), the Discharge and Threshold pins (6 and 7) are tied together and to the junction of a timing resistor and capacitor. The other lead of the resistor is connected to V+ and the capacitor's to ground.

As long as the Trigger pin (2) remains high, the IC will remain in its standby state, with the Output pin (#3) low (see the timing diagram in Fig. 2B). When pin 2 receives a falling edge or a negative pulse at least 1 uS in duration, the IC will go into the timing state. The output will switch high, and the Discharge pin (7) will float, allowing the capacitor to charge through the timing resistor until it reaches the 2/3V+ threshold level. The output will then again drop low, and the Discharge pin will clamp the capacitor to ground. If the Trigger pin is still low, the timing cycle will restart endlessly until it is brought high. For most uses, the addition of an RC differentiator network to the trigger pin will prevent this endless retriggering (see Fig. 6-12).

The monostable timing period is determined by the simple multiplication of the values of the timing resistor (in megohms), the timing capacitor (in microfarads), and the timer's inherent timing coefficient of 1.1. Therefore, for any combination of timing elements, the resulting timing period can be determined by:

$$t = 1.1R_tC_t$$

The practical lower limit of the timing period is about 10 microseconds; the upper limit, about 20 minutes. The limiting factor in the latter instance is the leakage of the timing capacitor, since the charging current of the timing resistor must be higher than the leakage current. Solid-tantalum and plastic-film capacitors are recommended for all timing-element use, due to their high stability and extremely low leakage. It is recommended that only metal-

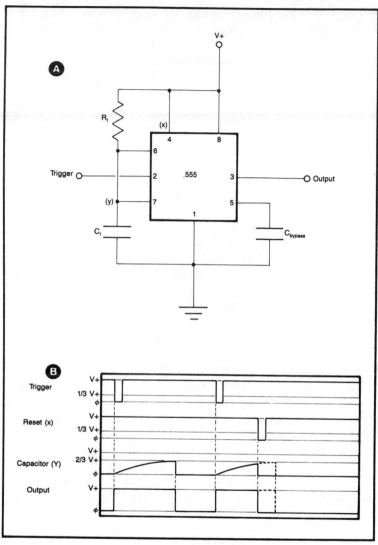

Fig. B-1. (A) A basic 555 monostable timing circuit. The timing period is determined by the values of R_t and C_t. (B) The timing waveforms of a 555 monostable.

film resistors be used for timing purposes, again because of their high stability.

Astable use of the 555 is just as simple, with the addition if a second timing resistor (Fig. B-2A). Timing resistor R_{ta} is connected from V+ to Discharge; resistor R_{tb} from Discharge to the

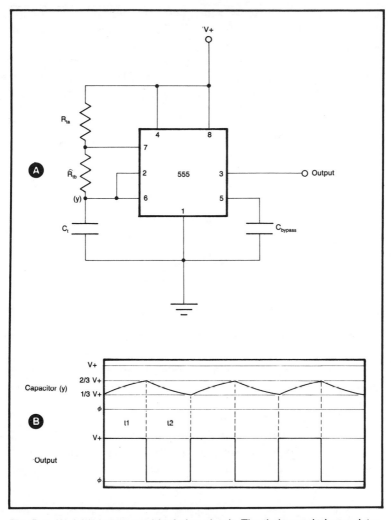

Fig. B-2. (A) A basic 555 astable timing circuit. The timing periods are determined by the values of R_{ta}, R_{tb}, and C_t. (B) The timing waveforms of a 555 astable.

joined Trigger and Threshold pins; timing capacitor C_t from them to ground.

When power is applied to the circuit, the output starts in its high state and the timing capacitor begins to charge through the two timing resistors (see Fig. 2B). When its charge reaches the 2/3V+ level, the output switches to low and the Discharge pin goes low. The capacitor then discharges through R_{tb} until its charge reaches the 1/3V+ level, at which point the output switches high and the Discharge pin again floats. The cycle will continue until power is removed.

The astable timer has two timing periods, t1 (the time that the output is high) and t2 (the time that it is low). The total time period of one cycle is known as T. The frequency, f, of the circuit is then 1/T. To calculate t1, t2, T, and f, use the following equations:

$$t1 = 0.693(R_{ta} + R_{tb})C_t \qquad\qquad t2 = 0.693R_{tb}C_t$$

$$T = t1 + t2 \qquad\qquad\qquad f = 1/T$$

Or, f can be directly calculated by the formula:

$$f = \frac{1.443}{(R_{ta} + 2R_{tb})C_t}$$

As with the monostable equations, R is in megohms and C is in microfarads.

555s can be used in another mode, not illustrated here: the half-astable mode. This configuration is identical to the astable, except that timing resistor R_{ta} is omitted, along with the connection to Discharge. The operation of the half-astable is identical to the astable with one difference. Upon power-up, the output will go high for a period determined by the monostable timing formula ($1.1R_{tb}C_t$). When the timing period ends, the output will drop low and remain there until the power is disconnected and reapplied. The primary use of the half-astable is as a power-up reset timer, or, in this book, as an exit delay timer.

Using the 556 timer is identical to the 555, with some pin changes, of course. The pinout of the 556 is as follows:

Function	Timer A	Timer B
V+	14	14
Discharge	1	13
Threshold	2	12
Control Voltage	3	11
Reset	4	10
Output	5	9
Trigger	6	8
Ground	7	7

Both the 555 and the 556 can have their inherent timing coefficient changed by using a resistor or a potentiometer between their Control Voltage pin and V+ to adjust the upper comparator's trip voltage (normally 2/3V+). The value of the pot will vary with the type of IC: the 555 will use a 5K; the 7555, a 1M; the L555, a 100K.

Using the specified pot, the timing coefficient can be adjusted from about 0.2 to 3.0 or more. You should experiment to determine the value needed for a desired change, and the pot then replaced with a metal-film resistor for stability. The bypass capacitor normally connected to the Control Voltage pin should not be omitted.

The primary reason for adjusting the timers' timing coefficient is to permit the use of smaller, lower-leakage timing components. One note: some timers may have trouble attaining a capacitor charge high enough to trip an extremely high-set comparator. Moderation and experimentation are called for when using this adjustment.

Index

Index

Index

OTHER POPULAR TAB BOOKS OF INTEREST

TAB | TAB BOOKS Inc.

Blue Ridge Summit, Pa. 17214

Send for FREE TAB Catalog describing over 750 current titles in print.